DONORICITY

DONORICITY

*Raise More Money for
Your Nonprofit with Strategies
Your Donors Crave*

STEVE THOMAS

LIONCREST
PUBLISHING

DONORICITY

Raise More Money for Your Nonprofit with Strategies Your Donors Crave

ISBN 978-1-61961-862-6 *Paperback*
978-1-61961-861-9 *Ebook*

CONTENTS

FOREWORD

BY JEFF GILMAN

Plato is often quoted as saying, "Wise men speak because they have something to say. Fools speak because they have to say something." I am so thankful that Steve Thomas wrote *Donoricity* because he's a wise man with something to say.

As a reader of *Donoricity*, I want you to know that if you communicate with donors or lead a nonprofit, you should take advantage of his wisdom.

I've been Steve's client for the last nine years. During that time, we have followed his thinking, leadership, and strategies. Before *Donoricity* was a book, it was what Steve and his crew provided for us. His agency, Oneicity, has been deploying this idea in the real world of our donor database and our donor development. What you're reading isn't just theory. I've watched our donors respond to this unique brand of donor-focused messaging in wonderfully positive ways.

What we've loved about his method is that it's not a rigid system that we have to fit into. Donoricity fits our voice and our situation. We didn't have to change who we are to see the results.

Over the years, I've seen the evidence that this idea works from a practical standpoint. We have the data that proves that this messaging creates an incredible sense of loyalty and a relationship that translates into donor retention and giving. I've seen it year after year.

Donors really do become more and more invested in our work. Steve's messaging creates a sense of genuine partnership. There's a measurable difference in how this strategy connects with donors. Donors truly feel a part of the work, not like they are ATM machines.

I think you'll be challenged and encouraged by what Steve has to say. You might wonder whether it really can work

to treat your donors so respectfully. After nearly a decade,
I can tell you, it does.

JEFF GILMAN
EXECUTIVE DIRECTOR
REDWOOD GOSPEL MISSION
SANTA ROSA, CA

INTRODUCTION

Donoricity?

What in the world does Donoricity mean?

Well, Donoricity means fundraising your donors love.

Donoricity means growth for your nonprofit.

Donoricity means always having engaging conversations with donors, even when they say they can't give.

Donoricity means direct-mail fundraising you're proud of.

Donoricity means a change in mindset you'll love (and you'll love how your donors respond).

Donoricity means donors are glad to hear from you (and glad to give to you).

Donoricity means that and more. That's what this is all about.

If Donoricity were in the dictionary, the definition might be something like:

[doh-ner-iss-i-tee] *noun*, the state of being focused on donors and donor desires; a growth strategy for nonprofits. It's like electricity or simplicity.

Yep, I made up a word to help describe what I have to say. The word might be made up, but the strategy is tested and proven. Donoricity isn't the first "-icity" name I've created. I named our ad agency Oneicity. More on that later.

First, let me take you to our offices. We have a piece of artwork by Hugh MacLeod[1] in our conference room that says, "You can't read the label on the jar you're in." The art is abstract, but the message is clear: You have to see your world through the eyes of others, and you'll probably need help doing it. This is where Donoricity begins.

---

1   Hugh's an amazing artist whose art changes the way you think about business and culture. Find out more at gapingvoidart.com.

We help nonprofits grow their revenue, primarily through fundraising. We want the art to remind our clients that it is a mindset shift to think first about donors. When you're inside the jar, your organization's goals may seem clear and primary. But what are your donors' goals? If you don't know, you run the risk of losing them. Donoricity changes how you think about and talk to your donors. Most importantly, it changes how your donors respond.

This is a powerful message for nonprofits struggling to connect with donors. Many of these groups are so focused on what *they* are trying to do that they don't take into account what *donors* want to do. What I've learned is that if you focus on your donors' goals, your work becomes more effective and rewarding. Fundraising becomes easier.

The worst mistake a nonprofit organization can make is to focus on themselves when fundraising. I know that sounds like crazy talk, but stick with me. It's a natural inclination to think of yourself first. You're committed to your cause, and the problems you are trying to solve are often large, so of course you need donors' help to fix them. Since you feel strongly about the work you're doing, it should be easy to convey that passion to potential donors, right? How can they not see the need to join in the fight with you? The struggle is real. As a result, nonprofits spend a lot of time selling their donors on the value of the organization's work.

They focus on the organization's needs, particularly its financial needs, and how donors can respond.

The problem is that most donors don't care that much about your organization's financial needs. Most donors don't care whether you are going to have enough money to make payroll this month or to publish your annual report or monthly newsletter. What donors care about is accomplishing something significant in the world. They want to fix a problem. They want to change their neighborhood, their city, their country, their world. A few donors will care about your organization's cash flow, but most only care about changing something in the world that is not working.

The trick for nonprofit groups is to jump out of the jar and see the world through their donors' eyes. Donoricity is a way to tell donors, "Here's the problem, and here's how you can work with us to solve it." If you do that, donors and prospective donors will lean in and pay attention. The focus is no longer on what *the organization* is doing; it's about what *the donor* can accomplish.

Most nonprofits genuinely believe they are donor-focused. But time after time, they make the mistake of not focusing on the donor and what the donor wants to accomplish. Instead, they focus on their own needs and finding help

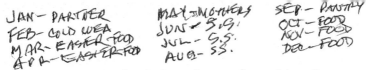

for the organization's mission. They can't see things from the outside, from where the donor is sitting.

The situation is analogous to what happened to businesses in the early 1980s. Back then, businesses recognized that if they focused on themselves, they wouldn't grow, and they would fail. When they focused on their customers' needs and interests, they succeeded.

Think about the retail giant Amazon. Remember when they just sold books and their competition was retailers like Barnes & Noble and Walden Books? By changing paradigms and thinking about what the customer wanted, Mr. Bezos not only changed the book and publishing industry, he revolutionized retail generally. His competitors aren't Barnes & Noble anymore, they're Target and Walmart and just about anyone who sells something to the consumer. How'd he do it? One easy answer is that he focused on what the consumer wanted and needed. Obviously, it's complex, but learning to think like Amazon is a smart strategy.[2]

Independent bookstores who've survived the Amazon tsunami are another facet to consider. They pay attention to their customers in a different way than Amazon.

---

2   In 1994 Jeff Bezos committed Amazon to become the "earth's most customer-centric company." I'm thinking he pretty much nailed it.

They don't have Amazon's big servers dishing data-driven recommendations. Local bookstores can build in-person relationships with their customers. Eagle Harbor Books is a small independent bookstore in my neighborhood. It's my wife's favorite place to buy books. It's not unusual for us to run into Drew, who sells her books, while we are standing in line at the deli getting coffee. They go back and forth with author recommendations and "if you liked that book, you'll love this book" kinds of conversations. This bookstore (and its people) focuses on its customers' needs and desires. It's *our* bookstore as a result.

In many ways, Donoricity is about making this kind of thing happen for your nonprofit.

Successful organizations are focusing on their donors' interests. Other nonprofits are focusing on the organization's needs and trying to persuade donors to write a check and stand aside so the organization can do the work. Who do you think has more engaged and enthusiastic supporters?

The more effective and sustainable approach to fundraising is to focus on what you already know the donor wants to do. If your organization's goals and your donors' goals align, you have a powerful match. You don't have to convince donors of anything; all you have to do is connect with them. It's easier for donors to give when they are already in love with the work you do, and you can show them what their contribution will achieve.

Donor focus is particularly important today because of the competitive landscape. Most nonprofits are so focused on themselves that they forget that there are tens of thousands of other organizations also trying to raise money. Donors are inundated with information about products and causes. Consequently, many groups have a hard time keeping donors focused on their organization and its needs. They can't be heard over the deafening chorus of "Me, too! Me, too!"

So, how do you make your voice heard over the din?

By crafting a message that resonates with donors who share your goals and who want to be a part of what you're working on. That's why it's important to be clear about who you are as an organization and what you're trying to accomplish. Only then will you start to see hands going up and hear people saying, "Well, that's interesting. I want to be a part of that."

Be clear about what you believe. I don't mean that in a religious or political sense. If you're feeding hungry children, you might say, "We believe every child needs, deserves, and has a right to three healthy meals a day." Donoricity will help you find the people who embrace these same principles. You can connect with them, and you don't have to convince them of anything because your beliefs are already aligned.

Donoricity is a marvelous way to make sure your voice is heard. Other nonprofits will be saying the same thing: look at us, look at us, look at us! "We do this or that and we need your money to fix this monumental problem." When you sound like everyone else, no one will hear you. But if you change the conversation to be about what the donor wants to accomplish, you will stand out.

At some point, almost every nonprofit has a board member or donor say, "You send out too many emails. You send out too many fundraising letters." But when you are doing donor-focused communication, you rarely hear that complaint (at least from donors). If donors like what you are doing, and they feel a part of your mission, they want to hear about it. If they've been part of a victory, they want to know about it.

This kind of communication helps you stand out and connect with donors. You're not just saying, "Me, too! Me, too!" or using a colorful logo or a glossy newsletter with big photos to distinguish yourself. Those tricks don't matter.

What matters to donors is that they connect with what you're doing in the world. You want to send the message that this is a collaboration, not a solicitation.

THE WINDING ROAD TO UNDERSTANDING

My wife, Kris Hoots, and I live on Bainbridge Island across Puget Sound from Seattle. Kris is my partner in all things.[3] She's a genius with data, analysis, strategy, and fundraising. Those of us who know her well get to call her Hoots.

Together, we own and operate two boutique advertising agencies. Our first agency, Oneicity (*wuhn 'i si tee*), helps Christian ministries with fundraising and marketing. Our other business, Hoots & Thomas, serves nonprofits (and a few small businesses).[4]

We deliver income solutions that help these organizations connect with donors and achieve their fundraising goals. We do everything from single, major-donor portfolios to completely integrated, multiplatform, annual development campaigns. We don't just pull these plans off a shelf; everything is custom built for each of our clients using the strategies and principles of Donoricity.

---

3   We're often referred to as Hoots & Thomas, both personally and professionally.

4   You can find out about our companies at Oneicity.com and HootsAndThomas.com.

We work with both faith-based and secular groups, and everything in this book applies to both types of organizations. I want to call to your attention that Christian donors have distinct values and motivations. We'll talk more about that as it comes up through the book.

If there is a direct path that prepares you to succeed in this business, I didn't take it. The trail I took was circuitous. In college in Texas, I fell in love with marketing and advertising and dreamed of becoming a J. Walter Thompson type of guy. My first job after college was working in the advertising and marketing department of the largest utility company in Texas.

It was a wonderful experience. I learned everything from television production to radio and print, but over time, I found the work to be empty. I left to start a business, and eventually, I had the opportunity to pastor and lead a couple of churches. I loved it, and my experience led to a consulting job helping a nonprofit with advertising, marketing, and public relations.

After six months, the nonprofit brought me on staff. I was director of operations for five years or so. This is when my fundraising education began in earnest. I was in charge of marketing and fundraising, among other duties. Eventually I served as their CEO for about five and a half years.

I hired ad agencies and consultants over that decade or so, and I learned an awful lot from them. I also learned a lot about what I didn't want to do.

For example, I had one consultant who would show up once a month and give me a list of all the things I needed to get done over the next four weeks. Then he would leave. He was a good guy and he helped me, but when he returned after a month, he'd ask, "How did you do on your list?" Then he'd start adding new things to my to-do list.

Finally, I got frustrated.

"So, you're getting ready to leave, and you've just added to my to-do list, and I have no one who can do all these things," I said. "Which of these things are *you* going to do?"

"I don't actually do the work," he said. "I help you figure out how to do it."

"Well, in that case, don't come back until I have everything done."

I fired him because I couldn't do all the things he wanted me to do.

The point is that I know people running nonprofits live

their lives with too much to do. When Hoots and I started Oneicity, we agreed that we would not just give our clients jobs and then walk away. We decided to practice "strategic doing"; we would roll up our sleeves and help our clients do the most strategic thing they needed. We are not the consultants who leave you with a list of jobs you don't have time to finish.

This is me [handwritten note in left margin]

Part of our work is teaching clients how to use a donor focus to improve their fundraising. Focusing on donors makes a nonprofit more efficient, and, in our experience, the results are much, much better. Anytime an organization raises more money, everything gets better.

AN EARLY REVELATION

Early in my career, I was the CEO of a nonprofit. That meant a big part of my job was making pitches to groups and major donors. I was horrible at it at first. I focused on my organization's needs and my needs as the leader of it. At least I was smart enough to know I wasn't good at it. So I tried different approaches and read books about how I should approach people. When something didn't work, I'd try a different technique.

No matter what I was reading or learning, I'd always end up saying things like, "Here's what we want to do. Here's what we're going to build. Here's what we're going to make. Here's what we're going to produce." People would hear this and begin to wonder how much it would cost them to get me out of the room. I felt like a really awful sales guy. There's nothing wrong with sales, but my job should have been to build relationships, not negotiate transactions.

Early on, I had an appointment with a businessman who, I had learned, was a person of significant wealth. That really was the main thing I knew about him: he was wealthy, and he had a loose connection to my organization's work.

He was an older Southern gentleman. He listened politely as I made my pitch. He had his arms crossed, and all I could think was that I needed him to give us a decent gift because that would really help our budget. I didn't say that, of course, but I know that was what came across. And as it did, I could feel the flop sweat starting to bead up on my forehead. It was clear that I was interested in his money more than anything else.

He was gracious, but then I got to the price tag. It's always tricky to bring up money on the first visit, but at least he was expecting it. When I was through, he smiled, and in that kind, lovely Southern accent of his he said, "Son, that's just not something I'm interested in." It was such a crisp, clear no.

This guy had plenty of money. I bet he could have reached into his petty cash drawer and pulled out enough money to fund my entire project. But he wasn't interested in what I wanted to do, and I wasn't interested in what he wanted to do. I was focused on me. I even made the mistake of bringing in what I thought were some slick brochures to help convince him. He was a multimillionaire accustomed to making multi-million-dollar deals, and I thought these materials would impress him. They didn't. I suspect that stuff had stopped impressing him many, many years ago.

I see fundraisers today make their versions of these same mistakes—not just in face-to-face meetings, but in public presentations. They get a group of people in a banquet hall and start clicking through the PowerPoint, and people want to get out of there fast. These nonprofit CEOs are talking about what they want to do. They're not talking about the people in the audience and what those individuals want to do.

Over time, I realized that I have a much better chance of engaging my audience if I am talking about a problem that they also consider to be a problem. Donors need a connection to what's in their heart. They want an opportunity to work on a problem they consider important. This is never going to be about color photos or PowerPoint presentations or logos or any of that stuff. That stuff can be helpful but should not be the main thing.

As I said, this gentleman was gracious. He didn't give me a dime, but he introduced me to some of his friends and helped me get a few more at-bats. I gradually learned to talk less about my organization's needs and more about the problems my organization was solving. I wasn't so quick to say, "Here's what you ought to do." Instead, I would talk about the problem and the opportunity we saw to solve that problem. That's when people started leaning in. That's when I realized that when I talk to somebody about something they are interested in, they want to have that conversation. They want to know more.

WHAT YOU WILL GET OUT OF THIS BOOK

This book will help you understand the theory, strategies, and benefits of Donoricity. You'll understand why it's important and why it works. I'll show you how to communicate with a donor in a donor-focused way.

I'll show you how to take a broad, strategic view and not get bogged down in minor details, like what color envelope works best for a direct-mail piece. I've actually had clients ask me about that. That really is the wrong question. The right questions to ask are "How do I write a letter to someone that focuses on their goals and not my organization's? How do I get donors to decide that, yes, this problem is something they want to work with me on? How do I get them to say they'll join me in changing the part of the world I am working on?" Once you've answered these questions, then you can talk about the color of the envelope if you really want to.

If you don't focus on the donor, your mailing will be just another letter in the mailbox, or email in the inbox, or commercial on the TV—along with everyone else shouting, "Me, too! Me, too!" You just won't stand out.

The other thing you'll get out of this book are some action-able suggestions and recommendations. Writing what I know and believe about Donoricity was a huge challenge. I'm used to talking with and thinking with clients who I know well. Or I get to engage with people in seminars who I get to know on the spot. Or I can have digital conversations on my blog. But a book is painfully challenging because you're not in a conversation with me. I don't know you yet. It's also been a huge wrestling match to decide what to include and what to leave out. So you can go to Donoricity. com and find resources and items that I decided not to include in the book but that you might find interesting.

One of the great things about being donor-focused is that

you won't have to change what's already in your heart. Everyone I know in the nonprofit sector is committed to the problem they are trying to change. Whether it's an environmental cause, helping children, or helping animals, we are all crusaders. We are all trying to make a difference in the world. Becoming donor-focused doesn't require that you change that. You remain true to your heart.

Many nonprofits get caught up in other concerns and forget to talk to their donors. A consultant will talk about what their brand should be or what their color palette should be. She will tell them to mail X number of direct-mail pieces or to send emails only on Tuesday mornings at seven o'clock. It's easy to get focused on that stuff and forget the goal is still to talk with their donors.

Imagine you have just one donor who writes one check a year that pays for everything. What an interesting situation that would be. You would be concerned about how that donor was feeling and thinking about you. You would treat that donor respectfully, and you'd be focused on that donor's goals. Plus you'd always spell their name right!

If you think of all the donors in your donor database that way, your focus shifts. The relationship becomes much different, much more meaningful. You don't worry so much about what the other organizations are doing or whether your logo stands out. You are interested in what that one donor wants to achieve and whether you are helping that donor solve that problem. When you look at all your donors in this way, your donor-focused messaging becomes distinct and sharp—and different from what everyone else is doing.

Chapter One

COMPETITION: WHETHER YOU LIKE IT OR NOT

A startling Yankelovich marketing study found that the average person encounters five thousand marketing messages a day.[1] That includes logos, brands, labels, and television advertising. It counts the little ads that pop up on the side of your Facebook page or embed themselves in your online bank statements.

When I mention this survey to nonprofit leaders, I can sometimes see that people in the audience don't believe me—it's too big a number. What I love to do is to cut that number in half to 2,500. That's still 75,000 marketing messages a month.

---

1   You can get the links to the study (and its critics) at Donoricity, or Google will find it for you.

Yikes.

Many nonprofits (and their boards) think they do too much marketing. But for many, your most aggressive fundraising is still a tiny drop in the bucket of messages seen every day by donors. Nonprofits often don't recognize how hard it is to stand out in this deluge of constant messaging.

Hoots and I call it the "Yellow Volkswagen Syndrome." Say you're shopping for a new, cute Volkswagen Beetle. Maybe a yellow one. How about a convertible? Once you begin thinking about VW Beetles, you'll start seeing them everywhere. It's not that there are more yellow Beetles on the road than before; it's that your awareness has been heightened. Everyone seems to have a Volkswagen Beetle!

That's how nonprofits look at their marketing. You're thinking about your marketing and fundraising. Because you focus on it, it stands out in your mind, and you begin to wonder if you are sending out too many messages. But what you see is not what the donor sees. Donors are seeing at least 75,000 marketing messages a month—really, twice that—and your message is one tiny piece.

To make matters even more challenging, most donors give to more than one nonprofit. So, they are also hearing from other nonprofits that are asking them to give.

Not only do donors forget about you, the organization they love, but they have other good-hearted nonprofits luring them away! Some of those other nonprofits have development and marketing budgets larger than your entire organization. This is the competitive landscape you are up against.

This barrage of messages reaches all adults, from Millennials to Baby Boomers and beyond. Don't believe anyone who says older people don't receive the same flood of marketing messages as young people do. They are receiving different messages, delivered in different ways, but the volume is the same for Baby Boomers and the Greatest Generation as it is for Millennials. Older adults may not be seeing as many messages online as Millennials, but they are receiving more through direct mail and television. It's nonstop.

This means your messages have to find a way to cut through the clutter and be memorable, or "sticky."[2] All sticky messages share certain things in common, and those things have little to do with colors or fonts. They have to do with how the message is designed. The best messaging puts the donor at the center of attention. It

---

2   I began using the term "sticky" this way after reading *Made to Stick* by Chip and Dan Heath. It's a great read.

communicates to the donor how they can make a difference in the world when they agree to work with you.

One of the nonprofits we support is called Love146. Their story is a perfect example of how sticky messages can work. This group fights child sex trafficking. Its cofounders came up with the name in 2002 when they traveled to Southeast Asia to investigate child prostitution. They were taken undercover to a brothel where children were being held captive. Posing as customers, the cofounders were taken into a room where they could look through a small window into a room full of girls, all between eleven and fourteen years of age. They were each wearing tiny dresses, and each girl had a number pinned to her chest. This is how customers selected the girl they wanted to rape. The girls were all blankly watching cartoons on a TV—except one. This girl was staring up at the window with an angry, defiant look. The others seemed lifeless, with vacant, sad expressions. But this girl still had life. She held her head high. Her number was 146. The cofounders decided this little girl was going to be one of their identifiers. They were going to love this little girl, this 146, and that was going to be what they called their work. Love146.[3]

When I do branding and messaging seminars, I'll use

---

3   Hoots and I support Love146 by not only telling their story but through financial gifts.

the story of that organization early in my presentation. Then, three or four hours later, I'll ask, "Hey, does anyone remember the name of that anti-sex-trafficking organization?" I have yet to see less than half the group raise their hands in recognition. Love146. They remember the name.

That's sticky, distinctive Donoricity branding. It has nothing to do with the organization's font. When you attach that branding to a donor-focused message and you say, "You can love little girls like 146. You can help them get out of the sex-slave trade," bingo. If donors are interested in this cause, it is a vivid, sticky, and actionable message.

It's been said, "We see things not as they are, but as we are." Our view of the world is shaped by our own perceptions and peculiarities. I'm not sure who said it first, but some variation of it has been used by many writers, from Anaïs Nin to Stephen Covey. I use this quote to explain why effective strategies are shunned by well-meaning organizations. Telemarketing is one of my favorite examples. Telemarketing can be a terrifically useful fundraising strategy for many organizations. But often, leaders won't even consider telemarketing on its merits because they personally don't like to be called at home, and therefore, they're sure no one likes a phone call either. I've seen organizations hurt themselves because someone said, "No one is reading direct mail anymore. Let's kill direct mail."

Making strategic decisions based on personal preferences will hurt your income.

You can make a difference for your organization by shaping your message, not by abandoning a certain strategy because you don't personally care for it. While telemarketing is tougher than ever, there are people who enjoy getting calls from the organizations they love. This approach can be very successful, but you can't just make a phone call. You have to have a donor-focused message.

OUR AVERSION TO COMPETITION

Nonprofits often don't talk publicly about their competition. It's kind of unseemly. It's natural for businesses to compete, but in the nonprofit world, where everyone is doing good and no one is motivated by profit, many organizations don't like to talk about other groups working on similar problems.

The truth is that you are competing against other nonprofits; you're competing for attention. To grow and thrive, you need to learn how to differentiate yourself.

As awkward as it is to say, this is particularly important when you are talking to Christian donors. Christian donors are often thinking about the blessings they receive from

God, and how they give is their response. If you are making a "Me, too!" case about how wonderful your nonprofit is, this won't have as much of an impact with a Christian donor as talking to them about what they believe God wants them to do. Christian donors are often thinking about how God will view how they use their money. They are not going to donate because you sold them or because you had the coolest strategy. Again, success comes back to having a donor focus. If you know donors are Christian and are motivated by a desire to please God, this knowledge can help you shape a distinctive message to them.

research — weak motive

For instance, environmental causes are not often thought of as Christian causes. Yet, if a Christian donor believes that he should be helping take care of this planet, why wouldn't he be interested in what you, as a traditionally secular cause," are doing? He should be. If he understands how he, through you, is going to be a good steward of this planet, then he is more likely to donate to you. The key here is not to appeal directly to this donor's Christian values but to his goal of making God proud. It all comes back to the donor, and what the donor wants to achieve.

LET'S TALK TERMINOLOGY

Before we end this chapter, let's get a couple of terms

straight. What's the difference between nonprofit and not-for-profit?

In my mind, the terms "nonprofit" and "not-for-profit" are synonymous. In our work at Oneicity and Hoots & Thomas, we use the term "nonprofit," and we refer to nonprofit organizations as NPOs. It's shorter, and it works.

But some people don't like the term, and with good reason. To them, "nonprofit" connotes a sort of failing, so they prefer "not-for-profit"—or some variation of that—as a way of clarifying that they never set out to make a profit. Others prefer to use the word "charity."

Throughout this book, I'll use the term "nonprofit" to include all groups—nonprofit, not-for-profit, and charity—who fit the IRS designation for groups that are not a business and are not trying to make money for themselves or stockholders. Everything I say in this book will be helpful whether you call yourself a nonprofit or a not-for-profit organization.

I also use the term "fundraising." Other people like to call it "development" or "advancement," but we call it "fundraising" because that is what you are doing: you're raising dollars. And I enjoy the clarity of saying we're raising funds.

Chapter Two

FOCUS ON YOUR DONOR, NOT YOUR ORGANIZATION

Earlier in my career, when I was the CEO of a nonprofit, we sent out a direct-mail piece to our donors explaining that we were experiencing a budget shortfall and needed their help. I'd like to think someone talked me into sending this message, but it was probably my idea. At the time, it made perfect sense: If you have a budget shortfall, you let people know so they can help you out.

A short time later, I got a call from a donor. He was a nice guy. He sounded older. He'd received our direct-mail piece.

"Help me understand what's going on there," he said.

I did my best to explain our situation.

"So, what you're asking is for my help to pay for your poor planning," he said.

Long pause on my end.

He was right. I was asking that. I didn't mean to be, though, and I would never have phrased it that way. In my mind, I was asking for help to continue doing the good work we were doing. But that wasn't the message that got through.

"Around here," the donor continued, "when not enough money comes in, we cut back so we don't get into trouble."

Awkward pause on my end.

He had a simplistic view of what was happening, but I could see why the donor would say it. I could also see that we had sent the wrong message in our letter. We had sent a message that was focused on the organization: "We need help paying the bills!" This was very important to the organization but was of little or no interest to donors.

This was one of those shaping moments for me. I realized I had done something dumb. Around our offices, we respond to a learning moment like this by raising our right hand and saying, "As God is my witness, I am not making that mistake again!" We usually call this a Scarlett O'Hara swear.

So, why do so many nonprofits use organization-focused messaging? I see it all the time. Part of the reason is tradition—that's the message they've always used. But I also think they send this type of message because it's easy. The people running the nonprofit are focused on their organization and on keeping the organization going. They can't separate themselves from the needs of the organization. So, when marketing or fundraising messages are written—even when they start out being focused on the donor—they lean towards what the organization wants to do. That's not as powerful as staying on message and focusing on what the donor wants to do.

What should you do, then, when you have a financial shortfall or you're not meeting budget? You look for a way to talk to donors that makes sense to them and that makes sense to the mission of the organization.

The mission of your organization is not to make budget. But a lot of nonprofits end up making this sound like their goal. They might throw in some donor-focused language or talk about what's important, but donors can tell that what's most important to these groups is making their budget. They are treating their donors like an ATM machine.

There was a time in the sixties or seventies when there were far fewer nonprofits—and fewer fundraising and marketing messages—and you could get away with focusing on money and still be successful. Not today. If you send the message to donors about your organization not meeting budget, you're going to be competing for attention with other nonprofits asking for help with problems your donor actually cares about. If an organization is asking for help to free a child from sex slavery and you're asking for help filling a budget shortfall, who do you think the donor is going to support?

Will your donors ever help you bridge a budget shortfall? Of course. But you have to be careful about how often and how you ask for that kind of help; donors will not tolerate those pleas very often. Violate this rule at great peril. If your messages are not as donor-focused and sticky as those of other organizations, you risk donors leaving you.

At this point, you might say to me, "Hold on! If we don't make budget, we don't exist." And, I would respond, "Why do you exist?" If the answer is to solve a problem or to change the world for the better, I would tell you to focus on that.

Talk to the donors about what's important to the donors. Say to them, "Here is the consequence if you don't participate: We may not be able to do sufficient work on this problem that we have been working so hard together to solve."   SOLVE ?

They'll listen to that.

WHAT IT MEANS TO BE DONOR-FOCUSED

Imagine a young, single man who goes to Starbucks on a regular basis and notices there's an attractive, young woman who is often there at about the same time. He sees her morning after morning, and after a while, he realizes he's attracted to her. She makes his heart beat faster, and his palms get a little sweaty.

One morning, he gathers his courage and approaches her table and asks if he can sit down. She's a little guarded, but he's a nice-looking young man, so she says it's OK.

"I notice that we're drinking the same type of latte," he says.

She looks at his drink and nods but doesn't say anything.

"I love lattes. It makes me think about the coffee my mother used to make. My mother loves me, and she's always thought I was this very special person, so she would make me this great coffee with steamed milk in it. She'd get up early and make me a cup, and it would be ready before I went off to school, and it was always really special."

The young woman looks at him quizzically but doesn't say anything.

He continues, "One time, I asked my mom if she would put some cinnamon in it, and she did. It was great! I loved it that way. But then one day, she added nutmeg, and that was even better! That's how I take it today—with a dash of nutmeg. I've thought a lot about it, and I think it's the nutmeg that sets off the flavor of the latte."

"What about you?" he says, "Why do you drink lattes?"

As she thinks about her answer, he says, "It really is funny how people think their choices are their own, but my mom always pointed out how our early childhood shapes our choices. She was a child psychologist. Very wise."

The young woman looks into the young man's eyes over her latte. As she draws a breath to answer, he says, "I monitor my caffeine intake very carefully. I've really been intrigued with how both the amount of caffeine and the timing of my meals impact my glucose levels. Of course glucose monitoring is critically important for good weight management."

"Luckily," he says, "You seem to be able to manage your weight pretty well. That gives me hope if you and I were to ever have children together. You'd help me make sure they eat right and take care of themselves."

The young woman carefully puts down her unfinished latte, gets up, and leaves.

Now it's the young man's turn to put on a quizzical expression. What has he done wrong?

This couple's story isn't going to develop into a love story. (It was painfully fun to write). I can't imagine how unpleasant it would be to live out, yet that's how many nonprofits act toward their donors. They're focused only on themselves with little or no interest in their donor beyond what the donor can do for them.

Nonprofits try to get a donor to fall in love with them by talking about themselves all the time. It's not that you shouldn't be self-revealing in a relationship, and it doesn't make sense to never talk about your organization to potential donors. But if you begin by talking about yourself and focus only on what your nonprofit is trying to achieve, you sound like the guy in Starbucks.

Look at it another way; we've all been in a situation like this. You're visiting with someone, and suddenly you realize you've launched into your third boring story in a row. You know it's time to stop talking and start engaging with the other person, but it can be challenging to stop talking about yourself.

One of the worst things you can do when talking with potential donors is to start teaching them about the problem your group works on. That happens a lot in public presentations by nonprofits; they're going to teach everyone in that audience something important. As soon as people in the room realize they are about to be lectured, they start looking out the window or glancing at their phones. You can almost hear them wondering how long this is going to take.

But if you can provoke curiosity or sympathy, or strike an emotional chord with the people in that room, then get out of the way because they will teach themselves. Donors need an emotional connection to an issue before they will listen to what you have to say about fixing it.

My wife, Hoots, is a voracious reader, and a couple of

years ago she read *Leaving Time*, a novel by Jodi Picoult in which one of the subplots involved a sanctuary for elephants who were retired from circus work. The book was fiction, but it turns out the elephant sanctuary is real. Hoots Googled it and learned that it's on ten thousand acres in Tennessee. Elephants have a hard life in zoos and circuses, but at this sanctuary, they can live freely and happily with other elephants. Hoots was emotionally impacted by this story. She learned that elephants actually have a wide range of emotions, and they value families and relationships. They're not dumb creatures; they recognize each other, and they visit gravesites of other elephants they knew. They're not simply animals that exist in the zoo or the circus.

You should know that, as a couple, we've never donated much to causes that didn't directly help people, but now elephants are in our giving portfolio. We support the sanctuary because of her understanding of this problem. It was something that struck her heart.

This group sends us their regular communication, an e-newsletter called *EleNews*,[1] and it's amazing. They don't talk about their organization, but they talk a lot about the elephants in the sanctuary. For example, prior to Valen-

---

1 Their print newsletter is called—wait for it—*Trunklines*. Nearly too cute, but I think works for them.

tine's Day, donors had an opportunity to buy valentines for the elephants. At first, I thought that was kind of corny. But the group followed up with a video showing these elephants, who all have names, receiving their valentines. There was Tange, delicately opening her box, and Sukari and Flora, who were shown stomping on their boxes to get at the treats inside. This may sound silly if you're not an elephant person. But if you are a fan of elephants, you say, "Oh! Look at what she's doing with that Valentine's Day gift! Isn't that great?"

The lesson here is that if you're creating messages for a nonprofit, you need to talk about your work in a way that offers donors entry points. You need to find that memorable and emotional sticky point—that thing that's going to grab somebody and make them say, "Well, I had no idea it was that way." This doesn't make that person a donor. But it makes them pause. If you can get them to pause, you've accomplished something that may pay off in the future for both of you.

Donors have to know the specific difference they will make or have made with their contribution. They may not want to know that they helped you get halfway to your one-million-dollar fundraising goal, but they will want to know that they helped feed Jimmy for a month in his after-school program or helped an Iraq War vet suffering from post-traumatic stress disorder get off the street and into a shelter. They need to know they helped an elephant rescued from a circus enjoy a box of treats on Valentine's Day.

Most importantly, you need to send the message that a donation helped the donor achieve his or her goal and not the organization's goal. When you send out an "urgent message to donors" that says, "We raised $560,000 last month to help people in need,"[2] the reaction is likely to be, "Wow, that organization is flush! Maybe they don't need my help in the future." But when you introduce them to the child they helped rescue from the sex slave trade, there is a much greater sense of accomplishment, and it's much more rewarding than seeing a big, impersonal number.

NOT SO FAST!

Another mistake nonprofits make is talking about themselves too fast. Let's say you are working on helping women who flee domestic violence. Don't start the conversation with potential donors by saying you only need $100,000 more to finish the dorm you are building for the women's shelter. While it may be important to you

---

2   True story. This email really landed in my inbox. An urgent message about raising
     half a million dollars without context caused me to wonder: Is raising $500,000
     urgent news? Is that good? Is it bad? Is it unusual? Why is it urgent?

and your mission, donors need something stronger and more emotional in order to connect with you. They don't need an artist's rendering of the dorm you want to build. They need to know what you are trying to prevent, what problem you are trying to solve.

You might start by describing how most abused women wait until summer, when their kids are out of school, to flee domestic violence. Many of these women will end up sleeping in their car because it's hard to couch surf with friends when you have two or three kids. You could begin by explaining that there is an estimated number of preschool students living in cars with their mothers in this one particular area, sleeping in back seats and washing up in gas station restrooms because they have no place to stay. It's a hard life. It's dangerous. Statistically, these kids who've endured this kind of life are at greater risk of being homeless, being abused, or becoming addicted to drugs later in life. And that's rough on the community. By telling this story, you establish the context for this dorm you need to build.

If donors love their community and they love kids and they have sympathy for women fleeing violent situations, they're now looking at your organization through a different lens. They're not thinking about a building. They are thinking about how hard it is for a kid sleeping in a car for weeks at a time. This isn't manipulative, but it does make donors look at the situation much differently. If I'm fundraising for the organization, I now have an opportunity to engage the donor in the emotion of the moment.

I'm never afraid to talk about money with a donor. But it's important to do it at the right time. If you've done a good job laying out the problem—if the person's involved (whether they actually say so out loud or not) to the point where they are wondering what it would cost to solve that problem—then you say, "It cost us $107,000 last month to house these women. What could you help with?" You may be talking about the money, but at that point, it's not about the money. It's about doing something specific, something concrete, with the money.

I push nonprofits to get to this: $ = X. I write those three symbols on the whiteboard and I say, "We have to get to this point. Dollar sign equals X." What that means is that once we've described the mission, once we've determined *1.* what the donor believes and wants to achieve, we have to *2,* be able to clearly answer the key questions: What will the *3* money pay for? What does it cost to feed the child? What does it cost to care for the elephant? What does it cost to rescue one little girl from a Southeast Asian brothel? You have to get to the concrete details. You have to get down to the cost of a single meal or a single night in a women's dorm. It may sound creepy to put a price tag on something like that, but it's critical. The donor sees a picture of a person in their imagination. They can picture a meal. The donor knows what $2.05, the cost of a single meal in your shelter, looks like. It becomes very real for the donor. And they know instantly how much they can help.

THE ROLE OF EMOTIONS AND RELATIONSHIPS

I'm not a doctor or a scientist myself, but I listen to things smart people say. One of those people is a neurologist named Richard Restak, who wrote the book *The Secret Life of the Brain*. Restak once declared that, "We are not thinking machines, we are feeling machines that think." Another favorite quote of mine is by poet Theodore Roethke, who writes in "The Waking" that "we think by feeling."

What these guys are saying is that we make decisions based on our emotions, not on factual information. Even if we don't think we are.

When a donor wonders, "Should I give to this cause, or should I look for a different cause to support?" that is the beginning of an emotional response.

When nonprofits tell donors about some kind of problem

they could help solve, the tendency is to lead with the statistics. That's a mistake. The best approach is to appeal to someone's emotions because that's the powerful motivator. You should know the facts and come armed with empirical data that supports the need to solve the problem. But it's not smart to roll that out until after a donor has already made an emotional connection to your cause.

One of the most important things I've learned over the years came from one of my mentors, who told me, "People give to people." What that means is you have to connect with people. You have to develop relationships with donors and connect them to your cause at the heart level. If you don't, you risk getting into a battle of facts, and these days, as everyone knows, facts can be disputed. There's always another set of facts.

Emotion, though, is truer than fact. If you have a feeling about something, that's your feeling. No one can dispute that. They can say you're wrong to feel this way, or they can say you should feel a different way, but they can't take your feelings away from you—it's how you feel.

This is why building relationships is crucial. This doesn't mean taking donors out to play golf and spending enough time with them that you become buddies and you feel comfortable asking them to donate. Rather, it means connecting with them as donors, knowing something of their heart, and connecting them emotionally to the type of problem they want to solve. The ask becomes more natural at that point. Whatever your communication channel is—whether it's an email or a website or a direct-mail piece—your message should be relationship-based. You need to build a human connection with donors and give them the satisfaction of helping to solve a problem they care about. In a relationship like this, the donor comes away thinking, "What I'm getting to be a part of is great!"

Statistics intimidate donors and reduce your fundraising effectiveness. Decision Research,[3] a research group in Eugene, Oregon, designed two similar fundraising pieces that featured a seven-year-old girl in a refugee camp. She was facing starvation. One group of volunteer donors received an appeal for donations that focused on the plight of this one young girl. A second group of volunteer donors received a similar appeal. It had the same story of the starving girl but also included information about the thousands of other refugees who were also starving. You'd think the second appeal would be just as effective as the first and possibly more so because of the statistics about the size of the problem.

---

3   You can read more about this at Arithmeticofcompassion.org or find my interviews with Dr. Paul Slovic on the Oneicity blog.

That was not the case. The people who got the statistics gave about half as much as those who only heard the story of the little girl.

If a donor can give $1,000, they can save this little girl. They can change that life. They feel great about the donation.

But if they get information that shows there are actually thousands and thousands of people who are starving, that donor calculates that $1,000 isn't going to help the problem very much. This feeling is discouraging. They feel conflicted because they might be able to help one person but not all those other people, and that doesn't feel very good. As a result, many donors will decide not to write that check.

It may seem counterintuitive when I say compelling statistics can discourage donors. But the effect is real, and this is why it's risky to focus on statistics. Instead, focus on the individual—the little girl you can save from starvation, the elephant named Tange that you can rescue from a hard life in the circus. If you are talking to major donors who want to help bring clean water to African villages, focus on the one village that the donors' $50,000 donation will help, not the hundred other villages that also need help. The goal is to help donors enjoy a solid, emotional connection to the problem they are helping to solve. For example, "Because of you, a family just like this will have a place to sleep tonight" or "Because of you, John, a forty-five-year-old laborer, now has computer training and a shot in the job market today."

Another mistake is what we call the Curse of the Expert.[4] You know so much about the problem you're trying to solve that it's difficult for you to explain it on a simple, human level for donors. As an expert, you feel the need to communicate the full scope of the problem. You may even find it challenging to imagine the basic questions.

This is beyond what the donor is interested in. The donor is thinking, "I want to help a person. I want to help an elephant. I want to solve a family's problem." You don't want to hide the numbers—the full scope of the problem—but you need to remember that the numbers are not going to be the motivation for most donors.

This is one reason why it's so hard for many nonprofits to become donor-focused rather than organization-focused. Nonprofits are usually not dealing with only one donor or one starving child or one African village that needs

---

4   One book that will help you move past the curse is *The Art of Explanation* by Lee LeFever.

clean water. They are immersed in their cause, and the temptation is to talk about this issue as they see it.

Another mistake is sending out communications that allow donors to feel like they are among a vast number of people you are appealing to. "You're one of twenty thousand people we're emailing today because we need everyone's help to solve this enormous problem." Donors may feel that you are not talking to them personally or that they're sitting in an audience. You want to break down that divide and make your communication more personal, like one person talking to another. Donors will know they are not receiving personal letters from you, but with the right language, the message will feel personal to them.

This kind of messaging is difficult to do correctly, which is why having an outsider look over your communications is so important. You can't read the label on the jar you're in, remember? Outsiders can see things you can't.

Chapter Three

PARTICIPATION: THE THREE ASKS

There are different ways you can enlist your supporters' help. I call these the three asks. And because it's the way one is supposed to create a structure, you can think about them as the three I's—income, involvement, and influence.

The **income** ask, of course, is financial. You're asking someone to write a check or donate through their credit card or transfer stock or pass on some land. It is a financial gift.

Most of the time, you and your donors are focused on the income ask, the money. That's logical, and it's what pays the bills, literally. We'll talk much more about this kind of ask. For now, just remind yourself that people have more than money. If you're building a relationship with a donor, you want more than just their money. The strongest relationships are built on more.

Involvement is another way to build that relationship. If I were doing three E's instead, I'd call this one "engagement." Involvement can happen a number of ways.

Take tour

Maybe you conduct a tour of your facility so a donor can see your operation in action. For example, Hoots and I visited a sanctuary for exotic cats that were rescued from unsafe or dangerous situations. We saw lions, tigers, leopards, and a bunch of other big cats. As part of the special cat-keeper tour, we saw how the sanctuary operated backstage. When a donor sees this, it validates her relationship with the nonprofit that runs the sanctuary. She sees what's happening. The critical component is to look for a way to

Engage

engage the donor during or after the tour. This group did a smart thing; they had contact information for national, state, and local representatives posted with a simple script for you to call your representative and ask them to help with a bill they were hoping would get passed.

Serve meal

Involvement can, of course, take other forms. One of our ministry clients invited some of their most generous donors to help serve a meal to people who were experiencing homelessness. These were donors of significant wealth. They probably didn't have much firsthand knowledge about poverty or life on the street.

Our client boldly decided to serve the meal restaurant style. The volunteers seated men, women, and children who'd lined up for the dinner at tables with tablecloths. They even had live music. My understanding is that there wasn't a dry eye in the room when the singer closed with "Somewhere over the Rainbow." I was told that the donors heard directly from the people they were serving about how beautiful it was to be served a meal and to hear live music. The expressions of gratitude and joy were constant.

Later, after the diners left, the volunteers sat down to eat together and talk about the experience. Many were emotional. You know that the next time the subject of the plight of the poor comes up, they will have powerful memories and mental pictures. They learned some things without being explicitly taught. They now have a nonstereotypical, concrete image in their minds of what it means to be homeless. And because we have to think about raising money, I imagine these donors will respond generously to an ask for their income.

In the faith-based world, the involvement ask might take a different form. For our Christian ministry clients, we ask their constituents if they would pray. Please understand, this isn't an artificial device or a gimmick. I personally know and believe in the power of prayer. I know that as I pray, God acts, and I know that He acts on me as I pray. It is a privilege and an opportunity to give something important like this to causes I'm attached to. It is a wonderful thing to ask a donor.

Plus, there's a delightful benefit when your ministry asks donors how you can pray for them. I'm always blessed and touched to hear how donors respond with heartfelt requests. This kind of relationship involvement moves past anything that resembles a transaction.

We have clients who ask donors to be mentors or tutors for the people the organization is helping. It's not a financial contribution, but it is important involvement, and these volunteers help the organization while building a strong, donor-focused relationship.

Influence is the third ask. This is where donors tell others about all the great work your organization is doing. Most supporters of your cause won't know how to share their influence unless you prompt them and give them a recipe. I like to call it a recipe to remind us all to keep it simple and step-by-step. You know how the best recipes break down complicated cooking tasks to simple steps? That's the best way to get your supporters to do this.

Social media is, of course, a great place for people to share influence. If a donor is active on Facebook, Instagram, and LinkedIn, he can like a post from your organization, and many people will see the post because of his click. This kind of influence lifts income.

[handwritten: post]

For example, imagine treating someone who is willing to spread their influence just like you treat someone who makes a financial contribution. Suppose the people running the Elephant Sanctuary came back to a donor and said, "Usually ten to fifteen thousand people see our posts but because of your click, sixty thousand people heard about the plight of one of our elephants. Wow. You made a difference with one click." Do you think that influencer will continue supporting the cause? You bet they will.

The three asks are not always distinct and separate. They often overlap.

For example, many arts organizations publish the names of donors and even include the amount of the donation. They may list the names of everyone who gave at the "Founder Level" and contributed $50,000 or more, then those at the "Supporter Level" who gave $25,000 to $50,000, and so on. There is a certain amount of ego attached to this, of course, but it's also a way of sharing influence. People looking at those lists might think, "Wow, those people are rich." But they might also think, "Wow, if those folks are willing to give that much, this must be a very worthy cause." Those original donors are contributing influence as well as dollars.

A similar overlap happens with involvement and influence. If you take donors on a tour and the last thing you ask is, "Would you be willing to post something—to Instagram or Facebook or Twitter—about your tour?" you are combining influence and involvement. You'll notice that my exotic-cat involvement example added influence at the end of their involvement. Combining asks maximizes engagement impact.

This is how Donoricity builds relationships. You are pulling people in and building a tighter and tighter connection with them. I believe that if you can get donors to respond to all three asks, you will have a closer emotional relationship with them than you would if they had answered only one or two of the three.

Donors may be temporarily out of money—that happens to people all the time—but they are never out of influence. Suppose you are sitting at a basketball game with a potential donor and you mention that it has been a very tough quarter for your organization and that you could use the donor's help. He tells you it has been a rough quarter for him, too, and that he won't be able to give until the of the year. If you drop the conversation there, you might feel bad. No one feels good saying no or hearing it. Instead, you can invite your donor to have coffee and help you talk to another potential donor. You can ask if he'd be willing to volunteer. Or you can invite him on a tour. He's contributing in a significant way, and chances are good he'll find a way to donate before the end of the year.

SCALING UP

Don't be afraid to say to donors, "Would you be willing to give a gift of $500 like you did last December?" You also shouldn't be afraid to say, "Here's a reason you might want to give a little more this year."

The truth is, if your organization is doing great work, your expenses are probably going up. There is always a need. And if you are doing a good job of communicating and validating the contributions of your donors, it's easier to convince them to become even more connected to your nonprofit. If you are connecting with donors on this relational level, donors are very open to giving again and very open to giving more. The key is helping them understand the difference they are making.

Almost all of your fundraising work is data driven to some

degree, so you will be constantly considering a donor's giving history and searching for opportunities to tell them how they have helped your nonprofit. Never pressure a donor—fundraising is not extortion—but we shouldn't be afraid to tell donors, "We know you're giving at this level. But if you gave more, it would help us accomplish this."

This scaling-up process also applies to involvement and influence. When your donors take a tour, they are giving you something very valuable: their time. In theory, everyone can make more money. They can earn or be given more dollars. But they will never get more than twenty-four hours each day, so if a donor gives you an hour or thirty minutes to come on a tour, they have given you something of significant value, something that's irreplaceable.

I keep mentioning tours, but there are any number of face-to-face events that can help you scale up. For example, our clients at the Redwood Gospel Mission have a job-certification program. People who have lost a job in one industry learn new, marketable skills that can help them land a job in a different field. One of these programs is called the Black Coat Program, in which trainees are taught how a commercial kitchen operates and can get a food-handler's license. Twice a year, the Mission invites donors to a banquet where they can hear about people whose lives they've helped change. Guess who does the catering? Of course, it's the people in their Black Coat program. This provides great experience for those in the program, and it allows donors to see the concrete results of their support. Donors tell their friends about their experiences, and they recommend to the Mission staff other types of industries that need trained workers. These donors get to become more deeply involved.

Here's another example of scaling up: One day, a Bible study group volunteered to serve meals at one of our rescue mission clients. Afterward, one of the women from the group asked for a tour and learned more about the programs and facilities the mission operated around the city. The next day, she asked the executive director of the mission if there was anything else she could help with. He told her about a capital campaign they had started for a new building. Was she interested in helping with that?

"Well, sure!" she said.

So, she began going around to businesses and meeting with individuals to explain to them why the Mission needed this new facility.

"I didn't raise much money, but I sure talked to a lot of people who had no idea how much the Mission was doing," she said later.

Eventually, the capital campaign was a success. The woman went on to become a member of the Board of Directors, and eventually became the chairperson of the board. And it all started with this woman's Bible study group helping serve meals one day. Not every donor who becomes involved with your nonprofit will end up on your board, but you never know.

Fair warning—I believe in a principle about involvement that might frustrate you. I believe you should never turn away someone who wants to volunteer. I know. I know. In principle that's a good idea, but practically, it's a challenge. People want to volunteer during the holidays when you have a limited number of spots available. Or people want to volunteer to do something you really don't need them to do. Or your work really doesn't have many needs a volunteer could cover. I know. I also know that just because someone volunteers, they won't automatically become a financial donor. But here's the truth: if someone wants to be involved and you can't or won't accommodate them, you've missed an opportunity to grow. I don't want you to miss any growth opportunities. So create as many pathways to create this kind of donor engagement as possible.

Chapter Four

FOUR-PART SCAFFOLDING FOR FUNDRAISERS

———

Oneicity serves a variety of clients, but rescue missions are a core element of our work. I admire the men and women who are called into this kind of ministry. It's challenging and difficult. As part of our service to create fundraising and marketing for these clients, we do interviews with the folks the missions are helping. Even though my role in our agency doesn't require it, I love to do these interviews. It's refreshing for me to hear how lives are being changed, and the interviews often provide insights for me as I lead strategies for our clients.

A few years ago, I had arranged to do some interviews for one of our rescue mission clients. I was interviewing a man who looked like he was in his midfifties. In the course of the introduction, I learned that although he had been through our client's program, he now owned and operated a successful small business. He was wearing a pressed and starched khaki shirt with his company's name on it. He was a very neat and pleasant-looking man. He exuded calm competence. In the first few minutes of chatting, he seemed like a guy I'd trust to fix or build almost anything: a house, a bridge, a computer...anything.

Often when I do these interviews, I begin by asking people, "How did you come to be at the mission?" Many times people begin by telling me what their life is like now. "I'm a different person," they'll say, or "I'm getting my family back," or "I've been sober for eighteen months."

That's important to know. But that's only impactful if we also know what their life was like before they entered the program, not after. That's crucial because potential donors can't understand an organization's effectiveness if they can't imagine what these graduates were like before they entered the program.

So, I asked the man, "What was your lowest point?" He described how years ago he woke up one morning in a dry storm drain just outside of Las Vegas. He was face down in the sand with two other meth addicts lying next to him.

He told me he crawled out of there thinking, "I'm going to have to get off drugs or it's going to kill me."

It was difficult to imagine this pressed, smart, and polite individual passed out in the dirt on the edge of the desert, but that is what happened. The impact hits you with great force: Only a remarkable treatment program could turn an addled, dirty drug addict staggering around the Vegas Strip into this crisp, competent man. The man in the khaki shirt was living proof of the program's value. If I were a potential donor, I would be asking myself, "Who do I make the check out to?"

BUILDING THE SCAFFOLDING

All effective fundraising messages for any organization have four components: **problem**, **solution**, **participation**, and **consequence**. In the case of the man in the khaki shirt, the problem is meth addiction destroying lives. The solution is an addiction-recovery and job-training program that helps those addicts. The consequence of not funding this program is that more promising people die in a storm drain somewhere instead of starting a small business and contributing to society. The participation part involves donors supporting the program in some way, such as by making a financial contribution. We dealt with some of the different aspects of participation in our last chapter on "The Three Asks."

These four elements—problem, solution, participation, and consequence—comprise the Donoricity fundraising scaffolding. To craft an effective message, you must have all four of these components. You can use them in any order, and they don't all have to be equally weighted in your message. But all four are needed to make your message powerful, sticky, and effective.

Donors also can quickly see the participation element. Most nonprofits are not shy about asking for participation, which, as we learned in chapter 3, can be financial support, involvement, and influence. But, as we'll talk about in the next chapter, many nonprofits struggle with describing the consequences of not addressing the problem. So hang on—more on consequence in the next chapter.

For now, let's look at another example of how the scaffolding works. Say your organization helps feed kids who are living in poverty. What are the four elements of your messaging?

The problem is that in the summertime, kids living in poverty often don't get the free school breakfast or the school lunch they need during the school year. They are often latchkey kids with little or no adult supervision, so in the summer they are also being deprived of the supervision and guidance that schools offer.

The **solution** is your organization's summer-school program. You feed the kids breakfast and lunch, and you send them home in the afternoon with a packed meal because there probably won't be a dinner waiting for them. You make sure that they are supervised during the day, that they have good role models, and that they practice their academic skills so they're ready when school starts again.

For the **participation** piece, you ask donors to contribute money. A contribution of $150 pays for one child's meals and supervision for the entire summer.

What are the **consequences** of not addressing the problem? Some of these children will be swept up by gangs, which tend to lure young, unsupervised children who are hungry for relationships and role models. These children have nowhere to go, so gangs—and the crime and violence that accompany them—become a part of their lives. Girls are swept up by gangs, too, or else victimized by sex trafficking or some other form of sexual abuse.

The problem and solution parts of fundraising scaffolding may be obvious. What isn't so obvious is how important it is to emphasize what is already being done. It's important to show that you have the expertise to fix the problem, that you're already working on it, and that you need the donors' help to maintain your momentum. Donors crave this validation, this understanding that they can help change the world. They need to see the momentum and the change that's coming.

Another value of this scaffolding is that it can help you hone your organization's mission statement. In my experience, most mission statements are useless (OK, that might be a little harsh, but you get what I mean). You and your staff spend a lot of time at a retreat pulling together some statements with the help of a facilitator, and then you print out your statement and put it in a frame and hang it on the wall. And that's it. You never refer to it. It doesn't do what you wanted it to do: guide your actions.

A lot of people get nervous when I encourage them to use such tangible, specific language in their scaffolding. I push hard to get them away from vague, general language, such as saying their organization wants to "fight poverty" or "end homelessness." Eliminating poverty or ending homelessness are lofty, noble ideals. But these are systemic problems that aren't going to get solved soon, if at all. But you can solve part of the problem. You can help get X number of kids off the streets in the summer

and make sure those children are safe, fed, a
When nonprofit executives articulate the four
their fundraising scaffolding, they can tell t
fresh, clear ways. The story is tactile, real, and
A donor will respond.

Problem — (STORY)
Solution — FFB - BOH - GFD
  PLUS
Participation - ask
  what their gift will do
Consequence
  IF WE DON'T HELP?

Chapter Five

CONSEQUENCES: THE DEFT TOUCH

For many nonprofits, describing the consequences of not solving a problem feels too emotional and possibly manipulative. It can feel like a scare tactic, and so they shy away from it.

But donors want to know what the consequences are. They need to know. If donors don't understand the consequences in clear, concrete terms, they may not be motivated to help you. Knowing the consequences of not solving this problem helps donors make good decisions about their participation.

Describing the consequences does require a deft hand, however. You don't want to overplay this element of the scaffolding. The actual consequences can be pretty grim: "If you don't support our program, this woman, this homeless mother of two children, will starve to death—probably tomorrow—if you don't give today. And starving is not a pleasant way to go, let me tell you." This may be true, but it's also melodramatic.

USING A DEFT TOUCH

Learning how to deftly deliver the right amount of consequences takes knowledge, skill, and practice. Our company describes consequences differently in a fundraising letter than it does in a newsletter. We use different language to describe consequences in an email than we do on a website. One size does not fit all. If you're in a face-to-face conversation with a long-time donor, you may need to do no more than allude to the consequences. The donor already understands the consequences. But if you're meeting someone for the first time, you might spend more time describing the consequences and less time discussing participation because you may not want to talk dollar amounts in your first meeting.

This is why you may need some help crafting your message. If you're not analyzing your communications, you can inadvertently overemphasize the consequences in your email, direct mail, or face-to-face communications. You cannot communicate consequences exactly the same way, all the time, with every donor. You become like that uncle we all have who talks too loud and stands too close; he makes you take a step back and look for an escape route.

One way to handle it is the fair-treatment explanation of the consequences. A fair-treatment explanation doesn't overdramatize the consequences, and it doesn't sanitize them either. In the case of the summer program, it's fair to say that if donors don't contribute, some of these latchkey kids will end up in gangs or working as prostitutes. You want the donor to say, "I didn't know how big a deal this was." You also don't want them calling you up the next week and saying, "I haven't slept in three days. I'm in therapy because you gave me post-traumatic stress disorder with your brutal description of the consequences."

Here's a personal example: I had the experience of crafting a program that helped young Romani children in Bulgaria. The Romani are also called Gypsies, and in Bulgaria, Gypsies are treated the way African Americans were treated in our country in the thirties and forties. The Romani have no rights and no advantages, and most are illiterate. They are not required to go to school or learn the Bulgarian language. As a result, many of the boys grow up to be thieves, pimps, or violent criminals. The girls often grow up to become prostitutes. I saw how long-haul truckers line up outside of truck stops in Bulgaria picking up these little kids. It was like a kick in the stomach.

The program worked this way: five- to ten-year-old Romani children could receive free lunch but were required to stay for literacy training. The idea is that these kids would never gain any economic advantage in that country if they didn't learn the language and improve their literacy. So, what is the fair-treatment explanation of the consequences of not doing this kind of work? One consequence is that all these kids will be hungry. But the larger consequence is that, without a program like this, these children will drift into a terrible life as criminals or sex slaves.

It was hard to explain to a charming, wealthy, somewhat sheltered, seventy-year-old American couple what the larger consequences were if this program didn't receive their financial support. They had to know this program was not just feeding hungry, disadvantaged children in Bulgaria. At the same time, did they need to hear all the grim details?

The goal of the fair-treatment explanation and the deft touch is to find the middle ground. It can be a mistake to delve too deeply when explaining the consequences. You don't want to shock or offend potential donors. It's far more powerful to sketch the outline of the consequences and let the donors' imagination fill in the details. The fair thing is to make your case and let them choose well with all the information you've provided them.

HOW TO CRAFT A CONSEQUENCES MESSAGE

Another easy mistake is making consequences too technical. We talked about the Curse of the Expert in an earlier chapter, and here's another place where that curse can rear its ugly head. Consequences don't always have to be simple, but when they become too technical, it's easy to lose your audience's attention.

For example, if you are working on bringing clean water to African villages, you could hold up a bottle filled with yellow or brown water and say, "This is the drinking water in the places we're trying to help." That's pretty effective.

But if you put up a PowerPoint slide with a list of the 150 bacterial agents and parasites found in the typical African village water supply and then spend the next twenty minutes talking about the dangers of specific organisms in the water, you're going to lose people. Your medical and technical knowledge might be impressive, but it will make sense to a very small number of potential donors. The rest of the potential donors in your audience will be bored out of their minds and maybe annoyed by this avalanche of technical information. They may even resent you for wasting their time with so much detail.

Many people, however, will be moved by the bottle of brown water. That image will stick with them. There's no need to go deeper than that. I might show that slide with the list of bacterial agents, but all I would say is, "This is a list of all the bad things we found in this village's water supply. It's bad, and kids will either die, or they'll never grow up to be everything they can be if they drink water like this every day." You clearly explained the consequences, and you backed those conclusions up with a glimpse of the research. You provided just the right amount of information to help these potential donors understand the consequences—and enough information to allow them to decide whether they want to participate in helping to solve this problem.

The key to crafting an effective consequences message is tailoring the message to your audience, whether it's a single person or a roomful of people or an email list. If you're appealing to a roomful of microbiologists, you might want to go into more technical detail about what's in that water. The audience might be impressed with your knowledge and may need that information to make a decision about whether to work with you to help correct the problem.

However, if you're at an event and you know 80 percent of the audience has never donated to your organization before and might not be familiar with your group's work, you'll make a different presentation than you would to a group in which 80 percent have a past relationship with you. For the group that is not familiar with your organization, you should describe the consequences with a low level of expertise and depth. That's using a deft touch.

DO YOU HAVE TO BE MANIPULATIVE?

A clumsy touch might be to show your audience of new donors a series of gruesome photos of the kind of birth defects that occur when pregnant women in this village drink that brown water. "How can you sleep at night knowing this is going on and you did nothing to prevent it?" you ask.

Yikes.

You would never do that, but the point is that you never want a potential donor to feel bad—even if they don't choose to help. Your goal is to make them feel exhilarated and hopeful that their donation can help solve a problem. Treat prospective donors the way you would want to be treated. I do not appreciate being made to feel bad or ashamed or guilty, and so I would never want to make a donor feel that way.

As I mentioned earlier in this chapter, most nonprofits are too afraid of appearing manipulative when they are describing consequences. As a result, they avoid describing the consequences or gloss over them. Doing this damages your chances of enlisting the help of many potential donors. Donors don't want to feel guilty, but they do want someone to help them understand what happens if they don't support your cause. You need to give prospective donors a concrete reason why they should help you.

I would not hesitate to say, "If your child lived in this village, you wouldn't let them drink this dirty water." But I'm not going to tell them that a child dies in Africa every six seconds and then hold up a ticking timer and say, "I'm asking you to give money to help solve this problem. Take your time deciding whether you want to support us. Uh-oh, another child died because you hesitated." I can get people reaching for their credit cards, but that approach is not right, fair, ethical, or sustainable. All anyone in that audience will want to do is to get out from under that pressure as soon as possible. They will never want to hear from you again because all they will remember is the pressure you put on them.

That's not the feeling you want them to have. You want

them to feel wonderful for helping these children get clean water to drink. You want them to feel amazed and enthusiastic because they are helping people and preventing some ugly consequences. That is sustainable. They will actually want to hear from you again. They're associating a positive feeling with you. And that's always a good thing.

They got to do something they loved doing. Who doesn't want to do some more of that?

DEALING WITH THOSE RELUCTANT TO GIVE

It's common for consultants to tell nonprofits that they can help organizations reach Millennials. Many donors have reached old age, and many nonprofits think they have to target Millennials to replace these older supporters. It's a cool youth and generational strategy all rolled into one. How can you not love that?

Well, it's actually a misguided strategy. *YES!*

What's far more effective is to make your message sticky and understandable and to put it in front of a large, diverse group that crosses all generations and to see who raises their hands to help. You want a message that people will remember—that's the sticky part—and you want a message that moves people. If some people are not moved, that's OK. There will be plenty of money from people who already love you or who fall in love with you when they hear your message.

Many people in the nonprofit world are chasing Millennials. I understand that it's an important generation because of how cause-focused they are. But as a broad age group, they haven't reached their prime time for giving yet. Disposable income is still an issue for them. Plus, that very strength—cause focus—can be a weakness. It appears they won't love your organization the way we Boomers will.

There is a large percentage of the population who will never give, and it doesn't make sense to chase people who aren't interested in your work. At the same time, you don't want people to feel ashamed because they don't support you. You don't want them to feel like all you are interested in is their money. So, it's important to stay connected to these potential donors to the extent that they will allow. Continue trying to connect with them, and remember that you are building a relationship, not executing a transaction. If you stay connected to these potential donors, there may come a time when you say or do something that will touch their hearts and convince them to participate.

It's also crucial to reexamine your strategy for reaching

lapsed donors—people who donated in the past but have stopped for some reason. If a lapsed donor is not giving to direct mail or has stopped coming to your events, try a different approach. Don't keep doing the things that aren't working; that's a recipe for frustration for both you and the donor (and it's literally the definition of insanity).

Instead, shift and use another channel. When you do this, it's not unusual for donors who have been lapsed for ten, twelve, or fourteen years to become donors again. When you're not asking for the same thing in the same way as you have in the past, you have an opportunity to reconnect with lapsed donors.

For lapsed donors, it often helps to remind them of the good they've accomplished in the past. You can say, "We just want you to know that you have made it possible for this good thing to happen." You don't have to say, "Of course, it's been twelve years since the last time you gave, and we could really use a check from you right now" because that shames them and makes them feel bad. Instead, you want them to feel warm again about the work they've done in the past. This is often enough to rekindle the relationship and make them an active supporter again.

There are occasions when it makes sense to let donors

know that it's been a while since their last donation. Most donors are busy people and typically have no idea how long it has been since their last gift. When you gracefully remind them, "Your last gift five years ago in February made a big difference," you can have a powerful impact on them. A reminder like this is not designed to make them feel guilty but to give them a time marker, and many donors will respond and say, "Wow, I can't believe it's been that long." That is an opportunity to rekindle that relationship.

During periods of economic downturns, you will hear from donors that they can't give because of personal financial troubles. They've lost their jobs, or they've lost half of their retirement accounts. One of the worst things you can do in that moment is to walk away from them. If you are building relationships with your donors—and not just conducting transactions—then it's important to remember that these relationships should flow both ways. When a donor can't give, express to them how you understand and that you still care for them. Many of our Christian clients do a great job of this. We coach and counsel how to do this by saying, "We understand. How can we pray for you?" Non-faith-based organizations can do something similar and say, "We'll be thinking about you" or "We're sending you good thoughts." You can also suggest other ways to give, such as volunteering or by using their influence to encourage other donors to find out about your work.

It's also important to treat lapsed or reluctant donors as though they are still on your side. When someone stops giving, many organizations assume the donor is mad at them. While, on rare occasions, that's true, most of the time it isn't. The truth is that the donor got distracted or forgot about you. To get them back, assume that they still love you. If you don't make that assumption, your own bad thoughts can seep into your messaging and create a tone that widens the emotional gap rather than closing it. This can make the donor feel defensive or embarrassed, and as a result, you can lose them forever.

For most nonprofits, the ideal approach is to craft a message that is sparkly, pointed, and spot on. Make sure your scaffolding is well constructed and then throw your seed out and see where it takes root. How quickly does it grow? Who responds to your message? No other messaging strategy works as well as this one. If your message moves them, donors—whether they are new or existing, lapsed or reluctant, Boomer or Millennial—will respond.

Not everyone who loves you can contribute as often as you might like, so acknowledge that and be understanding. You can also encourage donors to give in other ways, such as by volunteering or by using their influence to help you find new donors. (If you need to review, in chapter 3 we went into detail about how those contributions help your organization.)

Chapter Six

NO THANK YOU: THE RECIPE FOR DONOR RECEIPTING AND VALIDATION

When I graduated from high school, I got some gifts in the form of checks from friends and family. My mother had a rule that I couldn't cash any check until I had written a thank-you note for the gift.

That seems like a good rule, but I was a stubborn, stupid teenager, and I didn't get around to writing all the thank-you notes. I'm sure that somewhere there's the box with some of the uncashed checks because I was too lazy to write a thank-you note.

The purpose of the thank-you note in that context was to

acknowledge the gift, and most nonprofits take that process very seriously. So, you can imagine the expressions I get when I tell a roomful of nonprofit executives to stop sending thank-yous to their donors.

Their eyes roll back in their heads and their faces get red. It's heresy to suggest that they stop thanking donors for their gifts. Candidly, I sometimes secretly enjoy those moments.

I do it this way because I want to put a speed bump on their road—a barrier big enough that they have to nearly come to a stop to get over it. "Why," they ask, "wouldn't you thank your donors? That makes no sense."

After they've had a chance to fume and sputter for a few moments, I reassure them. Yes, you can say "thank you" to your donors, but don't make "thank you" the only—or even the most important—words in your communication. If "thank you" is all you say, you are missing out on an opportunity to validate your donors' gifts and develop a stronger relationship with them. Donors aren't giving because they want to get a thank-you note. They give because they want to change the world. They want to help a child get clean water. They want a retired elephant to have a safe place to live out its life. They want concrete results, so it's important to let them know what those results were. Their gift paid to transport an elephant to a sanctuary in Tennessee. Their donation bought enough to feed three impoverished children for a year. That's validation, and it's a very powerful message to donors. It has a far bigger impact than a simple "thank you."

A nonprofit named "charity: water" brings clean drinking water to people in developing countries, and the organization's leaders do an excellent job of validating their donors. During one of their live fundraisers, they put iPads at each table. As people donated, they could open the iPad and see real, live pictures of the people who would receive clean water as a result of the donors' gifts. At the end of the night, after the organization had reached its fundraising goal, the organizers showed a live shot of a well in Africa being completed because of gifts given that night.

Which is more powerful—a thank-you note for your contribution or a live video of clean water gushing out of a well that you paid for? Which message does the best job of saying, "You made a difference today"?

To me, there's no question.

Saying "thank you" is important, of course. You want to be polite. But "thank you" shouldn't be the focus of your communication. The focus should be on validating donors who made a very good giving decision.

This puts you into a conversation with the donors, and not just a transaction. A "thank you" ends the conversation. Donors are more likely to continue giving when they receive proper validation. You don't need just one gift; you need a lifetime of gifts from donors, so it's important to validate all of the different ways people contribute—whether it's income, involvement, or influence.

Think about it as though you're running an animal-rescue operation and you have volunteers who come in to help. If you tell a volunteer, "Emmit the pit bull became much calmer and gentler after you started sitting with him in his cage and petting him. A family came in and adopted him today, and I'm sure it's because you made him a much friendlier dog." Do you think that volunteer will feel proud and eager to help out more? Of course she will! And what do you think she's thinking of your work? She's excited. She's seen the difference. She's seen change. She's actually participated in the change.

RECEIPTING

The IRS requires nonprofits to send donors a receipt when donors make contributions (details on how to do this are in Publication 171, found on the IRS website at www.irs. gov/pub/irs-pdf/p1771.pdf). The gold standard for sending that receipt is twenty-four hours after the gift arrives.

But many nonprofits are so focused on the mechanics that they treat it as an accounting process, when in truth it is a donor-relations function.

You want to make sure donations are handled correctly, of course—that they go to the right bank and get deposited in the correct account and all that. But the communications that result from those donations are not primarily an accounting process. These communications are an opportunity to validate the donor's gift. This is a donor communication process.

We've successfully convinced several clients to move their receipting operations out of their business office and into their donor-relations department because that receipt is a valuable part of your relationship with donors. You want to keep the IRS happy, of course, but you don't want to squander a chance to assure donors that their gift brought concrete results.

HOW TO BE RESULTS-ORIENTED

I recently was asked to give an opinion on a charity that

was struggling to gain momentum in a fundraising campaign. The fundraisers would receive single donations, but donors were not continuing to give after that initial donation.

Although the group had an active cultivation program and was aggressively going after donors, the receipt and thank-you message was generic, with the same message going out to every donor. Donors were never learning specifically where their money was going or how their gift was helping. Consequently, donors felt little motivation to continue helping.

This demonstrates the importance of being results-oriented. Let the donors know precisely how their gift helped the cause. It's very important to be specific about how their gift helped because it reassures donors that they made the right decision to work with you. Their gift led to a concrete result. This makes donors feel good and improves your relationship with them. It's the epitome of being donor-focused.

Say you're running a summer camp for inner-city youth. Some of these kids have never been out of the city. They've never climbed a mountain or swam in a lake. So, when donors support your program, it's a mistake to send them a message that says, "Thank you for your contribution to our Annual Fund." Instead, send them a picture of Joey, the twelve-year-old from South Los Angeles. "Because of your donation, Joey saw the Milky Way for the first time. His biggest decision wasn't which gang to join but whether to put peanut butter on the top or bottom of his s'mores." That's very specific, and, for the donor, it's concrete and inspiring. The donor helped in a very specific way, and that made her feel good.

Some donors will continue to give even if their gifts aren't validated in this way. But you run the risk of your donors feeling they may have misunderstood the purpose of their gift. They may have donated to help build a softball field for the girls' varsity team, but when they received the same generic receipt that everyone else got, they might start thinking their gift went into some administrative pot to be spent on salaries. That's probably not what they had in mind when they made the donation, and it certainly doesn't motivate them to continue giving.

FAITH-BASED FUNDRAISING

The Donoricity validation process is especially important if you are a Christian nonprofit or if your donors are giving from a faith-based orientation. These folks often give because they believe God blessed them with the resources to give and because it is their responsibility to use those resources wisely. They need to know that their contribution made the world a better place. They want to feel as though God is proud of them for giving.

Christian donors are often even less impressed with thank-you notes. They are often holding themselves to a high standard for making a good decision on what organization to support. These donors may have little or no interest in whether you say "thank you" because they are focused on doing what is right for their community and doing what is right before God. And they don't want you to tell them that God is pleased with what they did because they might think, "Who are you to tell me what God thinks?" Giving is very personal and private for many of them, but they do need validation that their contribution was put to good use.

This is often referred to as a stewardship issue. Faith-based donors often think of themselves as God's stewards; God gave them their wealth, and donors have a responsibility to use that wealth wisely. These donors believe that God expects them to use their wealth in ways he values. Your thank-you note, if that's all you give, isn't going to validate their choice. If they gave you money to feed people and you don't respond with details of how you accomplished that specific goal, you may lose them as a donor. If a new charity comes along and convinces these donors that the new charity's mission is a better stewardship choice, the donors are going to support the new charity instead of yours.

Matthew 6:3 says that when you give to the needy "do not let your left hand know what your right hand is doing." This means that you should not make a big deal about your gift. You give privately, and you do not want public acknowledgment of your gift. This is why you may want to be careful about approaching a faith-based donor offering to name a building after them if they give you $100,000. That may not be motivating. It's no slam on them if they do like it. But don't assume.

I will say that Hoots & Thomas are listed on a Seattle theater wall as donors. We also love having our names on a plaque or two at the Wizard Academy in Austin. The Wizard Academy is magical place we're delighted to have our names associated with because of the work they do and how they go about recognizing donors. So the lesson is how you recognize your donors and how they feel about it.

Many secular nonprofits have a large number of faith-based donors. These nonprofits can't always tailor their messaging for that faith-based niche, but they should understand how important the feedback and validation portion of their communications is to these donors.

WORKING WITH CORPORATE DONORS

Many corporations support nonprofits by matching their employees' donations.[1] Employees donate and then fill out paperwork with their company, and later, the company makes its own donation to match the employees'. Corporations can support the causes their employees believe in.

The corporation, of course, needs an accounting. It needs to know its donation reached the right place. It's not an emotional transaction because you're dealing with a corporation and not a person, but you can thank the company and assure it that its contribution arrived. This is important to companies.

But how cool would it be if the nonprofit validated the employee's donation when she first made it and then validated the match a couple of months later after the corporation had made its donation? "Your company's match has arrived. Do you realize that you had twice as much impact because of this? Thank you so much for taking the time to match." You're validating the donation but also the extra time it took the employee to fill out the corporate paperwork to get the matching donation. The next time that employee gives, she's more inclined to

---

1   One option is to add a widget to your website that allows someone to check if a certain company provides matching donations for their employees. Oneicity and Hoots & Thomas use a widget from doublethedonation.com, but there are others, too.

remember the match and think, "Hey, I need to make sure to fill out that form again."

FEEDBACK FOR DONORS

Smart nonprofits are careful to always send donors specific feedback on what their contributions accomplished. It tells them how their gift made a difference.

Say you have a donor who helped you recruit people to attend a breakfast fundraiser. Your donor recruited his coworkers and neighbors and brought in twelve people to fill a table. Your response should be more than, "You filled a table at our fundraiser. Thank you." Instead, tell him that not only did he fill a table, but the people he brought in gave a hundred dollars apiece on average. Then you can say, "Your donation and your efforts to find new donors will let twenty-five underprivileged children attend camp this summer." This feedback loop not only validates their contribution but shows them how they made a specific difference.

Anytime you can do this, you're much less likely to have a one-and-done donor and will be more likely to build an ongoing relationship with them. What comes out of that feedback loop is a strong validation. Not only does the donor feel good when he gives the gift, but he can look forward to feeling good when he gets feedback about what that gift accomplished.

Validation like this sticks in a donor's memory in powerful ways, but many nonprofits undervalue it or bypass it altogether. So much attention is spent on getting that receipt out to the donor—the piece of paper for the IRS that says how much you gave and when and with all the right numbers on it—that organizations fail to acknowledge the good accomplished by the gift. This feedback is a way to help donors feel wonderful about their gift again.

This kind of feedback is important for corporate donors, too. Even when their contributions are matches of what their employees gave, these companies deserve to hear about the good their donation accomplished. You may have to report back to a company in a very factual, numerical way, but it's also important to include the emotion. "Your donation will bring wells to twelve villages in Africa where the women must travel three miles every day to a distant water source. The clean water you helped deliver will cut down on disease and child mortality by 75 percent." So the corporation gets what it needs—the numbers—but it also gets what it wants—the satisfaction of being a good corporate citizen.

Sometimes the feedback arrives through other channels

besides the mail. One client had a group of corporate volunteers help with a benefit in which the volunteers served food to disadvantaged people. Our client, a rescue mission, posted a picture on the corporation's Facebook page with a message, "Thanks to BigBucksSoftware's HR department for helping with our fundraiser. You helped fifty families have a meal this weekend! Our cooks were especially grateful. They said the folks from BigBucks-Software left the kitchen so clean that we didn't need to clean up after."

These volunteers could have each written a fifty-dollar check instead of spending half of their Saturday serving food. They can earn another fifty dollars pretty easily, but they are never going to get that Saturday afternoon back. They have literally given you a priceless gift—their time—so you have to validate it like it's a priceless gift. You don't have to overdo it and hand out plaques, but you do have to validate just how important their work was to your mission.

SO, DON'T SAY "THANK YOU"?

My goal here is to get you away from thinking that a timely "thank you" is all a donor needs. A "thank you" is not nearly enough. If that's all you say, your skeptical donors will think you're only grateful because you raised enough money this quarter to make payroll or pay the rent.

You need to give your donors feedback and validation. You need to tell them that people slept in a dry place this week thanks to them. Children got a hot lunch and a literacy lesson because they cared. A village in Africa has clean water today because of your generosity. A homeless family had its first real Christmas in five years because of the donation you made.

So, do say "thank you," but don't stop there. Make sure your donors understand what they have accomplished. They will feel the gratitude, not just hear it.

Chapter Seven

THREE TARGETS WITH ONE GOAL: BUILDING RELATIONSHIPS

———

Writing the next three chapters on your donor file,[1] recruiting new donors, and reactivating lapsed donors nearly did me in. At times, I thought I should just take them completely out. But these topics are vitally important—important enough that I could probably write an entire book on just those three challenges—so I knew I had to.

Think of your donor file as your bloodstream. It's what

---

1   I'll use "donor file" and "donor database" pretty much interchangeably. This is your list of donors. It can be an expensive, extensive piece of software or something simple. The point is it's the pertinent information about your donors: names, addresses, giving history, hopefully some biographical information, and other important details.

gives life to your organization. On one hand, it's pretty simple; if you don't have enough blood, you suffer. On the other hand, your blood is amazingly complex. It's got red blood cells, white blood cells, hormones, proteins, platelets, lipids, glucose, insulin, nutrients, and a vast array of other components that contribute to your health and vitality. This magical chemistry has to be in balance, and it has to be pumping at the right pressure to keep you going. It's complex.

If your donors continue giving year after year, and if you are successful with your organization's primary mission, the revenue will keep coming in and you'll actually grow. However, many nonprofit leaders err by focusing only on how much money is coming in. When you do that, you can overlook a problem that might be developing. If you never check your cholesterol levels and only think about your blood pressure, you could be in for a nasty surprise down the road.

For example, say you got $10,000 from your donors last year and $12,000 this year. That's good! But you also need to look at where that money is coming from. If you made $10,000 from one hundred donors the first year, but the next year, your $12,000 came from seventy-five donors, you may have a problem developing. You have more revenue, but you also lost twenty-five donors. Where did they go and why did they leave? It may feel like a comfortable strategy to raise more money from fewer donors, but if that trend of losing 25 percent of your donors continues each year, you'll find yourself in big trouble.[2]

That's why you have to examine those donors who leave you. Spend the time and money needed to get them back. The simple goal is to maintain the same number of donors from year to year, and of course, your larger goal should be to increase that number. The exception is when the donors you're losing are low-value donors. It's a good exchange to shed a donor who's never given you a gift larger than $20 in order to cultivate donors who are giving gifts two or three times larger on average.

THE THREE TARGETS

The Donoricity way is to think of your donor file as composed of three groups.[3]

---

2   Five years of an 8 percent year-over-year net loss of donors will cut your file by a third. I have a simple spreadsheet at Donoricity.com you can download and do some what-ifs.

3   I'm not including nondonors in this list. You likely have names of people in your database who have not given you a financial gift. These names might appear in your database because they are volunteers, have donated goods (Gifts in Kind, or GIK), or prospects. For our purposes in this chapter, I'm focusing on donors who've given a financial gift.

[handwritten: CURRENT / ACTIVE]

- **Continuing donors,**[4] the people who give regularly, year after year;
- **Lapsed donors,**[5] the people who gave last year but didn't give this year; and
- **New donors,** the people who have given their very first financial gift to you (one-time donors).[6]

COMMUNICATING WITH CONTINUING DONORS

[handwritten: ✓]

Retaining donors is one of the most important things you can do to grow your organization. Some organizations wrestle with 40 or 50 percent retention rates, which means *[handwritten: That's us!]* that if you have ten donors, only four or five will keep going year after year. That means you have to spend a great deal of money year after year just to stay even with the number of current donors you have.

Following the principles of Donoricity (using donor-focused messaging and concentrating on relationships with donors) often allows us to achieve retention rates 20

---

4   For simplicity, I'm only focusing on people. For more on businesses, foundations, and other nonpeople donors, see the Donoricity website resource section.

5   What constitutes a lapsed donor? Some organizations categorize someone as lapsed after a certain predetermined number of months. Other groups count the years since the last gift. The best way is to think in terms of complete periods—either a calendar year or your fiscal year. When in doubt, count calendar years because that's probably how your donor thinks of things. If they don't give in the last complete period, they're lapsed.

6   I mentioned "financial gift" because donors who volunteer and who donate goods (GIK) aren't in this category. These are only donors who have given their first gift.

to 25 points higher than some of the published national averages.

When nonprofit CEOs ask, "How do we keep donors?" they usually aren't looking for me to say, "It's relationship-oriented." Many times, I think they want me to say, "Here's a magic data trick" or "Here's a digital tool you can deploy" or "You need to buy our Millennial strategy." Tools and strategies are important, but they are only part of the process. Strategies that create relationships with donors are far more important, and relationships begin with respect. Validating gifts and providing donors with feedback is a way of showing them respect.

What you communicate about your work has to be calibrated to the level of your donor's involvement. New donors shouldn't receive the same messages or information as long-time, major donors, who are much more familiar with your work and might have an interest in the more complex aspects of that work.

The work most nonprofits do is complex. For example, treating drug addiction is a slow, complicated process. There are any number of reasons why people become addicted, and there are a wide variety of substances they can become addicted to. And addiction doesn't end quickly. Depending on your drug of choice, addictions can be very difficult to overcome.

If I have a new donor or a casual donor, I'm not going to take him into the deep end of the pool and spotlight the challenges of drug treatment. I'm going to talk to him about the scourge of addiction—the cost to families, cities, and society. I'm going to tell an authentic, sympathetic story of people who come to us for help, and I'm going to explain how we help them. I'm not going to get into the nuances.

However, the longer a donor is with you—the more often they raise their hand to help with income, involvement, or influence—the deeper you can go in explaining what you do. The more they understand the complexities of the problem, the more likely they are to see openings to help you solve it.

This approach works with any organization. Here's how it works with our rescue mission clients. Often, the easiest ask they can make of a donor is for a single meal. The donor can picture that meal, and they can picture someone who needs that meal. Maslow's Hierarchy of Needs comes into play here. Food and water are on the lowest level. The higher the ask is on the hierarchy, the more abstract and complex the offer. And that makes it more challenging for the donor to understand.

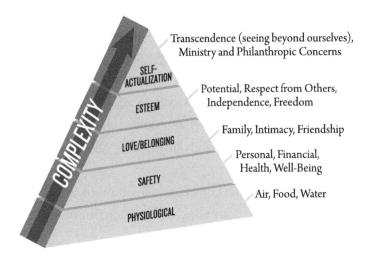

With other donors, you have the opportunity to go deeper. We often will create what we call "major donor paths" for donors who are giving at significant levels. This gives us opportunities and strategies to explain—in an email or digital or direct-mail piece—why we talk about meals so much. We'll explain that people who are dealing with heavy, hard things in their lives and don't know who to trust will come to the mission for a meal. They'll see people like them. They'll feel normal.

That may be the first step in a conversation with someone from the mission who can say to a person off the street, "If you ever want out of all this, we'd love to help. But even if you don't, remember that as long as you're hungry, we're going to feed you." We'll explain to the donor about the chemistry of drugs or alcohol and how malnutrition can change your thought processes. Two or three days of good food, without the stress of sleeping on the streets, can help someone think more clearly. They make better decisions. Some decide to change their lives. When you explain that complicated process to a major donor, chances are they will feel even more strongly invested in your work.

Generally, this whole book is about communicating with continuing donors, so enough about them for now. Let's examine lapsed donors next.

REACTIVATING LAPSED DONORS

Getting a donor who has stopped giving to give again is a challenge. It's certainly not impossible, but it's not an easy thing. The key to lapsed donors is to do everything you can to keep them from lapsing in the first place. I know that sounds frustratingly obvious, but it's true. First, start by doing everything you can to keep donors current.

Once someone loves you, it's crucial to maintain that relationship and not let them slip away. When you put your steely eyed accountant's glasses on, you can also see that it's worth it to spend money—perhaps more than you normally would—to rebuild your relationship with a lapsed donor.

When lapsed donors stop giving, they start a new pattern—a pattern of not giving. Your goal should be to find a way to interrupt that not-giving pattern and get them to give again. This is critical and easier to say than do. To get lapsed donors to break their new pattern, you often must break your pattern for communicating with them. If you normally communicated with that donor with direct mail, try using email. If you used email before, try using a phone call. If you've primarily been phoning the donor, visit him or invite him to an event. A donor saying no to one strategy isn't necessarily him saying no to you. It could mean that your old communication strategy no longer works for that donor. I think about it as pattern blindness. Remember: Predictable is invisible. These lapsed donors have been hearing and seeing the same things from you, and they have drifted away from the heart or emotion of your organization. So you need to break the pattern.

There are a number of ways to do that. You might use more pointed messaging. Make a powerful validation of their past gifts and include an emotional ask for a new gift. If you're using direct mail, you might make your piece look different from anything else they have received from you before. It might be smaller or larger than anything else you've sent. Instead of coming from the CEO, the communication could come from someone on your board. Many of our lapsed-donor strategies are built around the question, "How do I get this person to open this letter?" So, we'll use handwriting and make it look uniquely personal, as if it's never been touched by a machine.

You can also use data analysis to determine why a lapsed donor gave to you in the past. Were there topics or themes that resonated with them? Have you gotten away from using those themes? Perhaps it's time to return to them. The goal is to get them to break their pattern and reestablish a pattern of giving.

It's common for the donor communications we prepare for our clients, direct mail and email, to have lapsed-donor versions. This allows us to message uniquely to these donors. We talk to them as individuals as much as possible.

Steady communications with lapsed donors is the key. Don't give up. Don't get frustrated with them or with the time it takes. We'll spend more time on lapsed donors in chapter 9.

WOOING NEW DONORS

The only thing more difficult than getting a lapsed donor to come back is acquiring a new donor. Connecting with someone who's never given a gift has to be central to who you are and what you do. And again, as I've said before in this book, the best way to get and keep new donors is to build a relationship with them. Stay tuned for more on acquiring new donors in the next chapter. For now, let's talk about people who've become brand new donors—those are donors who've given you only one financial gift—their first gift.

When someone gives you their first gift, it's the beginning of a relationship. It's a huge mistake to treat them like all the other donors in your donor file. You really don't have a relationship with them yet. You may be shocked at how little they know about your work or your organization. You'll probably even be surprised at what they think they know about your cause. It can be painful to discover what actually motivated their first gift.

Connecting with new, first-gift donors shouldn't always be about donations. Remember the three ways people can give—income, involvement, and influence. This is true with new donors. While we are always looking for money, one of the ways to get money is by first getting people involved.

You don't go out on a first date and start talking about what names you want to give your future children. You don't want to sound like our poor friend floundering in Starbucks in chapter 2. But that's how a lot of nonprofits sound when communicating with new donors.

When communicating with new donors, don't overwhelm them with a flood of information. You can't expect a new donor to respond with a donation the next time you have contact with them. Just because someone came to your breakfast and heard your sparkling presentation doesn't mean they are ready to become a regular donor. And just because they responded to your new donor-acquisition, direct-mail piece doesn't mean they will become frequent givers. You have to be patient. You have to be willing to deliver your message again and again and not rush the relationship.

As with lapsed donor messaging, we frequently design messages created for these first-time donors. It's usually most effective to arrange your communications with new donors so that after their first gift, they receive your thank-you/validation/feedback pieces and then a newsletter. That sequence will help them come up to speed on who you are and how you're changing the world. It's ideal to use welcoming language in your communications so that they understand that you know that this is a new relationship.

Many organizations have what they call a prescribed welcome series or a new-donor series. It's a brochure or a series of messages or letters designed to elegantly grease the skids for the next gift. These messages are often not in print because that can be expensive and cumbersome.

Digital channels are easily automated, so these messages can be dripped out to a first-time donor. These messages allow you to tell a story and help your new donor get oriented and comfortable, at which point you can offer them a tour or invite them to an event. You might say, "As one of our new partners, we'd love to show you around. Click here to let us know when you'd like to come."

A new donor isn't really a donor until he or she gives a second time. A first gift is often based on a tenuous, fleeting emotion. That's not a bad thing; it will give you the opportunity to grow a relationship. But remember the bond is fragile between a new donor and your organization.

That's why your messages to first-time donors should focus on building that bond. Acknowledge that they are new to your organization. You shouldn't act like these new donors are supposed to already know everything. You don't want your newsletter to sound like a stranger's family Christmas letter in which everyone is identified by their first names or nicknames and there are vague references to past events as though everyone should remember them. Longtime major donors don't need to have certain things explained to them, but new donors might. Welcome new donors. Invite them in.

Woo those first-time donors slowly. Don't rush them or take them for granted. Give this new bond time to form.

THE SECRET TO ALL THREE GROUPS

A big part of building this relationship with donors—whether they are continuing, lapsed, or new—is taking them back to the emotions they felt when they gave their first gift. You may not be directly asking for a donation, but you are reminding donors how good it felt when they donated in the past.

You might say, "Here's something that happened that could not have happened except for the giving you have done." Maybe a client from your treatment center has just started a new job. "You may not remember them, but I told their story in a newsletter last quarter. They were sleeping in a storm drain three years ago, but they've been with us for the last two years, and yesterday they started a new job as a foreman on a landscaping crew." You're not asking for money. You're not saying, "You're the big fat ATM, and I'm coming to you with my debit card because I need cash." You're saying, "You're making a difference, Mrs. Donor. I know who you are, and you are important to us."

When you communicate this way, you're connecting donors back to why they gave and validating what an amazing thing they did. It's not a simple "thank you" but an acknowledgment of what they accomplished and the difference that they made with their gift. It can become a back-and-forth communication. It becomes this dance that the nonprofit gets to do. The organization tells stories of need and validates success, and the donor gets to share in the excitement. This kind of communication becomes very powerful because in many situations you become friends with the donor after you've bonded around this cause. You're connected. The donors know their value—not because you told them but because they see it. They hear it. They experience it.

Chapter Eight

RECRUITING NEW DONORS

If getting current donors to remain active is the most important task in your world, then finding and recruiting new donors might be your most difficult task. Acquiring new donors has never been cheap or easy, but today the task is more challenging than ever before. In fact, anyone who claims they can provide you a cheap, easy, and guaranteed solution to finding new donors might also have a nice perpetual motion machine you could buy.

Instead of buying in to their fun fantasy, stay with me in reality.

More nonprofits and ministries are competing for your donors' attention and support than ever before.

There are more marketing messages competing for your donors' focus than ever before.

There are more channels and strategies to connect with donors than ever before, and more are added nearly every day.

And people have more control than ever before over which marketing, advertising, and fundraising messages they receive.

That's the cold reality. As much as I wish it were different, there are no magic bullets. There are no easy answers.

But there's hope. Real hope that can produce results you'll enjoy.

This hope isn't about cheap and easy. It's about relationships. It's about thinking and knowing the right strategies. Donoricity will help.

First, let's be clear: your goal and sole focus in recruiting new donors must be to make an emotional connection.

Potential donors have to understand the problem and relate to it before they will be willing to support your work.

A good example is how Hoots and I became involved with Taproot Theatre Company, a nonprofit theater group in Seattle. We became aware of the group when they asked for a consultation with us, and as we became more involved, we learned about the nonprofit's efforts to raise awareness of bullying in elementary and middle schools in Seattle. The group uses the power of drama and role-playing to help students understand how they can intervene when they witness others being bullied in school. When we learned about this program, we became more involved with the group as donors and volunteers. This was an issue that we felt strongly about, and it caused us to lean in. We've supported the program for over seven years now, and I'm actually on the board of directors for the group.

That's how you get a new donor.

We didn't donate because we like theater, although we do. We donated because we felt an emotional attachment to their antibullying campaign.

Nonprofits spend too much time telling strangers what their organizations do and why the organization is so good at it. They use staggering statistics to show the enormous scope of the problem they are working on. They use these frightening numbers in an effort to drive home just how urgent and severe this problem is. And, after all that, they wonder why none of these strangers send them any money.

The problem is that donors look at those numbers and they get scared off. The donor wonders, "How is my little donation going to make a dent in a problem that huge?"[1]

Instead, your goal in recruiting new donors should be to make an emotional connection with them.

For many nonprofits, forging this kind of emotional connection is difficult. There is no magical technique for achieving it. There are effective strategies, however, and donor-focused messaging using Donoricity is critical to succeeding.

New donor acquisition is expensive; it takes time and frequency. It won't happen as quickly as you'd like, and most people will need to encounter your messaging more than once before it will register enough for them to make a good decision about becoming a donor.

You have to take the long view. You can't get discouraged if they don't immediately reach for their checkbook. You're still getting to know each other. If they come to an event or volunteer at a function or donate some food or goods, that's the beginning. Those are the people who can become financial donors. You're just trying to find an opportunity for them to say yes, because when they

---

1   Again, refer to Decision Research's study on the Arithmetic of Compassion.

make that first donation, you now have a chance to validate their contribution. This gives you the opportunity to draw them closer.

AVOIDING THE CHURN AND BURN

It's also important to stay true to your mission. It's not worth muddying up your image or your mission in order to raise money or attract new donors. This approach is not sustainable, and it can actually cause damage in the long run.

A few years ago, we had a client—let's say they were a substance-abuse treatment program, because I need to disguise their identity—that had hired a well-meaning national ad agency to help them with their fundraising. The agency was aware of how much Americans like to feed hungry people around Thanksgiving, so they talked the nonprofit into focusing its fundraising message on its need to feed its clientele and the neighborhood. Remember, this is a substance-abuse program; their central mission is to counsel these addicts and get them through a recovery program to help them return to productive lives, not to feed them holiday meals. While they did feed people, it was not at all what a reader of the direct mail would have imagined went on. But that was the message they sent out to potential donors.

The campaign performed very well. They found new donors. The problems showed up in the next year. When the nonprofit went back to these donors to get donors' help funding its addiction and recovery program, the donors weren't interested. They had given money to feed people. They really didn't care about people struggling with addictions. They just wanted to help someone at Thanksgiving. So donations fell off until Thanksgiving rolled around again and the nonprofit could trot out its annual feed-the-hungry plea. These donors would lapse and then be reacquired or reactivated by the holiday feeding fundraising blitz.

That's "churn and burn." The program had to keep finding new donors to replace the ones they had burned with their deceptive campaign.[2] The nonprofit was finding new donors, but it was paying to reacquire these same donors over and over and over. It was expensive and a complete waste of resources. As we began our work with this client, it was a significant challenge to help them solve this problem they'd created.

You can't ring psychological or emotional bells that are not part of your mission. You can't have a relationship with

---

2   I nearly didn't use this story because I was afraid you'd think the agency that caused the problem was mine. It wasn't. We came in to help figure out what their problems were after the damage had been done and to help build a strategy to fix the problem.

someone who thinks you do one thing and then finds out you actually do something else.

WHERE TO FIND NEW DONORS

When you are trying to find new donors, look for people who are most likely to care about the problem you are solving. Not everyone will love your cause as much as you do. In fact, the harsh reality is that most people won't care or notice. That's the sad reality.

So it becomes a numbers game to find the people who will care. There are several good strategies all based in getting your message in front of the right people. Let's talk about your message first. If your messaging isn't right, it doesn't matter who sees it—you're wasting your time.

GET THE MESSAGE RIGHT

When communicating with nondonors (donor prospects), keep it simple. You won't have very much time to make an impression, so don't get bogged down in the complexity of your issue. You can't be boring, dry, or consumed with minor details.

Focus on the donor's desire to change something in the world. This is where the scaffolding we talked about in chapter 4 comes into play. You must grab the donor's attention and coax them into your story. The donor must understand what you're asking, what the need is, and what the consequence is if this problem isn't tackled. You're not trying to make them feel guilty, but you are telling them a story with emotion. A narrative, as we'll find out in chapter 10, draws people in a thousand times faster than facts.

The facts don't matter.

OK, facts do matter, but not as much as you think. A compelling story will win the day. Throwing facts at people, or describing an enormous, entrenched problem, only risks driving people away.

Instead of focusing on stats or facts, tell the story of one person, one animal, one community, one neighborhood. Bring the problem down to a human scale. Make it clear what can be changed by action and what will continue if no action is taken. Think back to Love146. Remember that one girl with the defiant expression? Of course you do. You heard that story and remembered the problem of sex-slave trafficking in Southeast Asia. You could imagine her expression. That story stayed with you.

That's how your story should be.

When you focus the problem on a human scale—the plight of an individual, for example—you create an emotional response from a potential donor. The donor might think, "There, but for the grace of God, go I." They remember the near misses in their lives. "If things had gone a different way, I could be homeless...I could be poor...I could be addicted." They remember when someone helped them out of a tight spot. Most of us can find those events in our memory, so your message to the potential donor could be, "You could be the one helping this person the way you were helped." That's not making them feel guilty, but you are tapping into what it felt like for them to be pulled out of a horrible situation. They feel fortunate to have made it through, and the strength of that emotion compels them to lean in and look for ways to reciprocate. It's their turn to rescue someone.

The story must keep the donor at the center of the narrative.

Cultivate the donor's satisfaction in changing something, in joining a group of like-minded crusaders, or in participating in something they care deeply about. If you are asking them to donate money for backpacks for underprivileged middle-school kids, remind them what it felt like to be an awkward middle schooler. If you want them to donate money for sports facilities for kids who don't have them, remind them how they had to take a bus into the next town to find a baseball diamond.

Tap into the donor's emotional fabric. We can't know all of what's in that fabric, but we can help them imagine how good it's going to feel to give a warm bed to a little girl who fled an abusive home with her mother and slept in the back seat of a car for three months.

The facts, presented alone, will block that emotion. Don't focus on large, insurmountable problems, like world hunger; potential donors look at a massive problem like that and think their donation wouldn't even put a dent in it. That's not a satisfying thought. Facts and staggering problems force donors into an analytical state of mind that seldom leads to a donation.

We still have to have the facts. The facts are for the business partner or the spouse or anyone who wants to know why the donor wrote that amount on the check. The donor might use the facts to justify their donation, but that's only because the emotions that really prompted the donation are harder to explain.

Remember, facts lead to conclusions. Emotions lead to action. You want action.

FINDING THE RIGHT AUDIENCE

Once you have your message right, you're halfway home... but only halfway.

I consistently get asked about how to do direct mail, new-donor acquisition. I'm responsible for millions of pieces of direct mail for new-donor acquisition. It works. But it only works with the right message and the right audience. It's tricky, technical, and not for the faint of heart.

So don't think about direct mail first, think about ugly babies.

I love imagining the look on your face reading that. Stay with me.

Have you ever run into a mother with her newborn baby in the grocery store or an elevator? She's cooing and smiling at her little bundle of love. You lean over to look, and there's a little red, squash-faced, really ugly baby. A little Winston Churchill without a cigar. You see an ugly baby. She sees the love of her life. You don't see beauty. She can't believe you don't see beauty.[3]

Take a deep breath. Your nonprofit is an ugly baby to most

---

3   I always get in trouble when I talk about ugly babies. Don't judge me; just learn the lesson. And try to remember that I really do love babies, ugly and otherwise.

people in the world. Most (not many, *most*) people will have absolutely no idea why you are doing what you do and why they should help support you. The issue of finding the right audience is recognizing that much of the population won't be interested in what you're devoting your life to. The wrong strategy is to assume that the right message will overcome this problem. It'll help, but it won't solve it.

You have to find the right people. And that's where it can get pretty complicated.

If you're a start-up or a small nonprofit, you almost certainly will need to stay away from direct mail for new donor acquisition.[4] It'll cost too much, and the ugly-baby syndrome will keep it from being profitable soon enough. You certainly will find people who will take your money to do direct-mail, new-donor acquisition for a small organization, but odds are you won't be happy with the results.

So what do you do?

If you're small, there are two great strategies: in-person and digital.

In-person donor acquisition works like this: you get people who love what you do to help gather people who they

---

4   We'll talk specifically about direct mail in chapter 11.

think will love what you do. Then you tell your story and help them understand how they can join you in changing the world.

Events can be amazing donor acquisition tools if you stay focused on the purpose and if you are careful about how much time and money you're spending to put on the event. For more on event fundraising (and event-driven new donor acquisition) go to the Donoricity resource page.

Events aren't easy or automatic, but nothing in donor acquisition is.

Digital channels work wonderfully well for nonprofits of all sizes. Social media (Facebook specifically) lets people who already love your work connect you with their friends. You can deliver your message much like you would at an event, but it's online instead. Please note that social media isn't typically a good place to ask for donations; it's the place to tell your story. (See chapter 12 for more details on using digital channels.)

If you're sure you're ready for direct mail, then you have to find the right people to mail. The right message to the wrong people won't do you any good. Finding the right people is a bit of a science and a bit of an art.

You can find companies who will help you do some research to try to discover who to mail. Again, hire someone committed to results.

I've worked on projects where the clients wanted to recruit only major donors. The only criterion was that the people have great wealth. This is a painfully flawed strategy for at least a couple of reasons. First, people of great wealth often hire gatekeepers, administrative assistants, or business managers to keep people they don't want to hear from at arm's length. The reality is that charities and nonprofits are often in that category. Wealthy people defend themselves from pitches of all kinds.

The second and most important flaw is this: Knowing a person's income or even their history of giving to other charities gives you no insight into what is in their heart or whether they would emotionally connect with your work. This approach also leaves out wealthy people who purposely live modest lives so they can support the causes they love. I frequently say that a donor's wealth or upscale address is not a measure of their philanthropic intent.

You need to know more about a person than his or her income.

There are several strategies to deploy, but what works is

to use your current donors to build a profile of potential donors. There are ways to use what you know about your donors to find other people who match them in terms of demographics and behavioral patterns. We've been seeing very encouraging results from this kind of data work.

How much modeling you do depends on the medium you're using. In digital platforms, you can use a great deal of specific modeling. But in direct mail, it could be too costly to do detailed modeling—depending on the size of your audience and the scope of your project. You also run the risk of shrinking your audience too much and not getting in front of as many people as you need to make the numbers work for you.

Since I don't know your unique situation, I can't give you specific recommendations. But if you get your messaging right and then remember that most people won't love your baby, then you'll be on the right track as you pursue new donors.

Chapter Nine

REACTIVATING LAPSED DONORS

———

Donors will leave you. No matter how good your communication is or how successful your organization is at accomplishing its goals, donors lapse and stop supporting your efforts. It's inevitable.

Nationally, nonprofits lose almost half their active donors each year. Your retention rate might be higher than a recent national average of 46 percent,[1] but it's likely that you will lose more donors this year than you expected to. Even donors who have supported you for decades can leave for one reason or another.

———

1 I'm not a huge fan of metrics like this since there are so many variables that affect them. But many people want some kind of number to measure against. The 46 percent number comes from the Association of Fundraising Professionals. Tracking your year-over-year retention rates is a better metric.

LTDV

Some groups identify a donor as <u>lapsed</u> when they've <u>stopped giving for two years.</u> Others will consider a donor lapsed if they miss one year. What's important is that you're consistent with the time frame you use to identify lapsed donors and that you have a <u>clear definition of what constitutes a lapsed donor.</u> Know your important donors and their rhythms. When a major donor who has been giving to you quarterly suddenly misses two quarters in a row, you don't want to wait two years to call them personally to check on them.

<u>Identify lapsed donors as quickly as possible.</u> Our research shows that the longer donors remain lapsed, the harder it is to get them back. So, identify them early and adjust your communication to restore your relationship. If you wait too long, they may forget about you and move on to another cause.

Every donor is precious.

You don't know what is in that donor's mind or the sacrifice they've made to give what might seem like a small gift. Christian ministries will remember the widow's mite (Mark 12:41-44). Remembering the donor's perspective and sacrifice keeps you focused properly.

Also, you have invested a significant amount of time and

money in your relationship with them, and you don't want to lose that investment. You've already taken them on that long journey from not knowing who you are to knowing all about you. They are a valuable asset but also a friend who once loved you, so it's worth the effort to get them back. Don't give up on them too quickly.

WHY DONORS LAPSE

There are many reasons why donors lapse. If you're a local organization working on geographically limited issues, you can lose donors when they move away. You can still keep them as supporters and donors, but you will probably have to communicate with them differently, and you may not be able to count on their involvement or influence as much as you did when they were your neighbors.

Some donors lapse because they lost their jobs or their investments tanked. Continue to communicate with them. They may be willing to help in other ways as a volunteer or in spreading the word to friends about your good work. This kind of involvement and influence is as important to your organization as financial donations.

Treat your donors, particularly your major donors, the same when they don't give as you do when they are giving. You want them to continue feeling valued and included.

Remember, donors love to give more than their income. When money is tight, ask for their involvement and influence. When their fortunes turn around, these donors often come back joyfully because you continued to show how important they are to you.

Some donors lapse when they retire. Many nonprofits are dealing with older donors who reduce their giving because they are worried they won't have enough money to support themselves till they die. It's a problem for nonprofits, but it's also an opportunity to talk to these donors about making your organization a beneficiary of a portion of their estate. This is often the largest gift a donor can give.

Donors are lured away by other groups. We see this happening to organizations using "set it and forget it" communication and fundraising. These groups send out the same types of messages on the same platform year after year. Donors lose interest and drift away to an organization with more dynamic stories to share. Some groups cut back on communications with donors to save money, and that's also a mistake. Even when some donors only give around Thanksgiving or Christmas, studies show that they need year-round reminders of your important work. When they don't hear from you, they wander off to another organization.

HOW TO THINK ABOUT LAPSED DONORS

When donors lapse, many nonprofits think they somehow drove them away. They think the donors are mad or no longer believe in their cause.

That's rarely the case.

That can happen, of course. The donor reads something negative about your nonprofit in the news, there is a major change in your organization's leadership, or your group alters its philosophy in a way the donor dislikes. But this, too, is rare. It's typically a small percentage of people who become upset about these changes.

Lapsed donors can be brought back. They loved you once, and a quick phone call or personal email can sometimes rebuild the relationship. This kind of communication can be done by a real, live person, or it can be part of an automated campaign.

A bigger problem is a phenomenon I call "pattern blindness." This is when you send the same direct-mail fundraising letter, digital newsletter, or brochure over and over again, yet the donor doesn't respond. Sometimes the secret is to break your own pattern and shake things up. Redesign your newsletter (this is often a great tactic when newsletter results are slumping). Make your annual event a dinner instead of a breakfast. While it's essential that you stay true to your mission, brand, and message, it's just as important to surprise and delight your donors.

Many lapsed donors don't realize how long it's been since they last gave a gift. Years ago, I was involved with a project for a client, and I interviewed lapsed major donors. I found that almost all were still enthusiastic about their group's work. When I asked how long it had been since their last gift, most thought it had been only a year or two. But when I told them how long it actually had been—some hadn't given in five or six years—they were surprised or shocked. They weren't cognizant of how much time had passed.

This reinforces the need to stay in touch with your donors and study their patterns. Some only give in April. Some only give around Christmas. Some only give every other year. It's important to understand their pattern and connect with that pattern. Don't assume that because a donor only gives once a year, you can cut out all your direct-mail letters, newsletters, and emails. We've tested this, and we know that donors need frequent communications to keep you in their minds. If you ask a donor whether they would like you to cut back on your communication with them—unsubscribe them from the newsletter, for example—most donors will say yes because they want to save you time and expense. But that's a mistake. What's best for your organization and your donor is to continue communicating with them as much as they will allow.

Avoid making lapsed donors feel guilty or ashamed. Nobody likes being made to feel that way, and neither do your donors. If they tell you that they can't give, let them know that you understand, and that you'd like to stay in touch. If you are a Christian nonprofit, you can offer to pray for them or ask them if they would pray for you. If you are a secular organization, you can express your concern.

Lapsed donors need to know that you still value them, still care about them, and want to stay in touch with them. Most donors will allow that. If you can stay in contact, you have a chance to keep them until things turn around and they can give again. If you break contact and turn your back on that lapsed donor, you really don't have a chance of getting them back.

You can acknowledge that it may have been five years since they last gave a gift, but never connect their absence to some kind of financial problem with your organization. Instead, let them know how important gifts are and how they allow your work on a problem to continue.

Try to reconnect them to what they first loved about your

organization. If they first donated to the children's library, remind them how important those gifts were and how that program still needs help. It could be that they thought the children's library was no longer something you worked on. Maybe you stopped talking about the children's library in your newsletter in recent months. So circle back and try to tap back into that origin story—their first love—and get them excited again. It's like a couple returning to the restaurant where they had their first date. It's a relationship you have with your donor, so connecting back to those emotional anchors often allows them to rediscover their passion and remember how good it felt to give.

When our clients use these donor-focused strategies (the Donoricity way), we're finding that their retention rates stay impressively high. Higher retention rates result when groups understand their donors, spot their patterns, and adjust communications to keep from losing them. If your organization had a 55 percent retention rate slip down to 50 percent or 40 percent, you need to find out why. You might need some help. That kind of downward trend can often accelerate. What starts out as a small leak can become a dangerous flood. It's not really about the national benchmark—it's about how your nonprofit is doing year to year.

Chapter Ten

TELLING THE STORY: MESSAGE CRAFTING

Stories have the power to communicate great truths. That's why when Jesus was asked "who is my neighbor?" he didn't respond with a list of criteria. Instead, he answered with a story of the Samaritan who shows mercy to an injured man. Great communicators and persuaders are storytellers, and you have to tell stories, too.

As Maya Angelou once said, "People will forget what you said, people will forget what you did, but people will never forget how you make them feel." That really illustrates the essence of Donoricity messaging. While your words and actions are certainly important, how you make donors feel with those words and actions is paramount.

Stories can set fire to emotions. The desire and motivation to change the world comes from emotion. Facts, with few exceptions, don't create emotions. I don't have to know very much in order to question a fact or to reach an incorrect or contrary conclusion about a fact. But a story is much different. A story draws me in, awakens my feelings, and motivates me more than facts.

A story has heroes, conflicts, and villains, and it usually has a plot. Heroes encounter difficulties as they journey to their goal. It could be that your story has some central, important characters, such as the person who needs to be rescued, or the organization founder who discovered the problem and rescued the victims.

But when I'm telling a story for a nonprofit organization, I invite the donor to step in and experience the emotion of having already given the gift. Donors have to see themselves in your story before they decide to help.

To get to the point of wanting to take action, donors often have to see how bad the problem is. Think back to the man in the khaki shirt I talked about in chapter 4. Before he became a competent, hardworking entrepreneur, he was a drug addict lying in a storm drain on the edge of Las Vegas. I had to see that image in my mind before I could fully appreciate the recovery program he graduated from.

Donors need that. Unless they've seen the problem unfold (either firsthand or in their mind's eye), they are not ready to ride over the hill and save the day. But once they have that picture, it's easy to see themselves as a hero—or at least in the cavalry riding to the rescue. I don't want to overplay this hero thing, but you must nurture the donor's passion. You want your donors to think, "I'm going to participate here. I'm going to change things to the extent I can. I'm the kind of person who does this sort of thing. And that is going to feel amazing for me."

When crafting messages, shift from telling someone "you should give this gift" or "you should help this cause" to persuading potential donors that they are, in fact, the type of person who rides over that hill. Let the donors see themselves as heroes. When that happens, they're not making a decision about giving a gift. They are making a decision about what kind of person they are. Once they've done that, it's time to ask, "Well, then, what kind of help do you want to give?"

Crafting a message with an implicit question like, "Are you the kind of person who helps in these situations?" is a powerful approach. It puts the donor at the center of your story. You can tell a story about how your founder discovered a problem—the founders of Love146 who traveled to the brothels of Southeast Asia are a good example of that kind of story—but you have to give donors a chance to say, "Yes, I am that kind of person." You don't come right out and tell them they're that type of person. You let them decide.

This is essential in new-donor acquisition and donor cultivation. Let them decide whether they want to enter the story. Once they become a donor, you'll know they are that kind of person. This knowledge allows you to sharpen future communications with them.

Well-crafted messages lure donors into a larger narrative. That story might be how your organization got started: You saw a tragic problem that broke your heart, and now you are working to solve that problem. You're looking for others who share your compassion. Potential donors see how they fit in. Sometimes the story is about the victim, and again, donors can see how they can help rescue that person. You are not selling them on an idea so much as you are letting donors slip into this driving, forceful narrative.

Your story must be concrete and vivid. The more donors can see the colors, feel the heat or cold, and smell the odors, the better they will remember it. That will lead to action.

One of our clients was the CEO of a shelter for abused

and homeless women and children. These women and children were coming out of addiction, extreme poverty, abusive situations, or all three. Our client told us how he visited the shelter one Christmas morning. Pancakes were sizzling on the griddle and coffee was brewing in the urn, and as he entered the dining area, a six-year-old boy left the dining table and came running toward him. The boy threw his arms around the CEO's leg, and said, "This is the best Christmas I've ever had!"

The CEO's staff teased him about how often he told that story. They'd all heard it a dozen times, so an inward groan would go up whenever he started to tell it again. But I encouraged him to continue telling it. "Tell it whenever you can," I told him. The story's rich detail stirs emotion and has a powerful effect. What must your life be like when the best Christmas you've ever had is in a homeless shelter? Can you imagine? It's the kind of story that gives a donor room to picture herself being a hero to that boy. You can also quickly understand that there are probably many other little boys in the world not enjoying their Christmases this year. Maybe you could help.

Organizations that are not donor-focused have a hard time telling stories like this. They seem to be afraid to tell a story. They are afraid that their story isn't strong enough, so they resort to using numbers and throwing facts around. There is little emotion to it, and donors aren't drawn in. Donors need to feel strongly about your work and their role in it, and the best way to achieve that is by telling stories.

ADVICE FOR THE CREATIVE SIDE

Seth Godin has written this wonderful book called *Purple Cow*, which is about how organizations and companies need to differentiate themselves from their competition.

We all know what a field of regular cows looks like, and you wouldn't pay attention to it if you were driving past. But if there's a purple cow standing out in the field with all those Holsteins, you are probably going to pull over and take a picture because you've never seen anything like that before.

You need to consider that purple cow in your communications. What do you do that no one else does? If there are others who do the same work, how do you work differently? You don't want to brag or put anyone down, but you need to find a way to stick in people's minds.

Our brains are wired to notice changes in familiar patterns, but if it's the same pattern over and over again, the brain learns to ignore it. Organizations need to be wary of their own repetitive communications. You have to remain true to your mission and your central message and brand. But you also need to <u>add unexpected twists</u> that <u>keep your donors engaged</u>.

GIMMICK OR STRATEGY?

I've been quoted as telling people, "One person's strategy is another person's gimmick." If you're doing something because everyone else is doing it or because you think you are supposed to, it's probably a gimmick. But if you're doing something for a good reason and you know exactly why you are doing it, it's a strategy.

An example of this is using a person's name in a letter or some other communication. This is a very effective strategy if you do it right. Even donors who are just scanning your letter will spot their name in it. But if they see it over and over again, they start thinking you are like the used car salesman who feels the need to use it in every sentence. It drives them crazy and comes across as insincere.

If you know what you're doing, you will use the technique with greater care. <u>You should only use the name at the most powerful moment in the letter or email—right in the paragraph that you are most interested in having the</u> potential donor read. This might be a call to action or something else, but if there is one paragraph in that letter that you want to make sure the potential donor reads, it's this one. So, that's where you put their name. Done right, that call to action becomes a direct, personal appeal to the donor.

That's a strategy. Repeating a person's name without understanding how the science works is just a stupid gimmick.

We see this with typography, too. Either there is nothing bold or underlined in a letter, which is a tragic mistake, or there is way too much bold and underlining, which is also a tragic mistake. If you know the brain science and creativity strategies behind it, you know when to use bold and underline as a way to grab a person's attention. It's not a gimmick but a strategy.

READERS ARE REALLY SCANNERS

The best way to imagine a potential donor reading your printed material is when they are glancing at it just before tossing it in the garbage or feeding it into the shredder. Most readers will only scan the material, so you need to get your message across quickly and include unpredictable elements that will catch their attention.

Some people think that if people are not reading printed

material from beginning to end that your printed piece is not effective. The opposite is true. People will read at least some of your printed content if it's designed properly. Even when your printed piece isn't read completely, it can still be effective in changing a donor's behavior or influencing his or her actions.

Infographics are a good way to grab attention; they quickly convey meaning without forcing donors to do a lot of work reading. Think about infographics as today's headlines.

However, even eye-grabbing typography or the strategic use of the unexpected is no substitute for creativity and thoughtfulness. You can't be predictable, and you can't do what all the other organizations are doing. It's important to be heartfelt and respectful.

Keep in mind that you are not your donors. Just because you don't like something doesn't mean it won't work for you. For example, if you don't like getting telemarketing calls, don't rule out using telemarketing for your organization. The truth is, some donors love to get calls and are happy to give a gift over the phone.

Thinking your donors and potential donors are just like you (and your friends) is one of the most painful mistakes I see people make. If you base your donor development, fundraising, and marketing on your personal preferences, you will not connect with very many people, and you will not raise much income.

MAKE IT PERSONAL

As I said earlier, the goal with all your communications is to be as close to one-on-one with your donors as you can get. In an ideal world, you could have face-to-face talks with all your donors. But since that's not feasible, all the other tools—from direct mail to email to social media—should honor your goal of talking to each donor individually. You craft messages for many, but they should still sound very personal.

Use your donors' names when it's appropriate. If I go by Steve, don't address me as Stephen (seriously, I'm a "v" not a "ph"). If all I've ever given you is fifty dollars a year, don't ask me for ten thousand.

Your database of donors and their activity should have enough rich detail to help you make this one-on-one connection. You should know how long your donors have been with you, when their last gift was, and what time of year they gave. If this knowledge is reflected in your communication, donors will feel like you know and care about them.

Chapter Eleven

DIRECT MAIL

———

Many people think direct mail is dead. They call it "snail mail," and they think it's an antiquated approach that costs a lot and doesn't pay for itself. What's more, they think no one reads direct-mail pieces anymore. Or they think that the few who do read direct mail are not good prospects as donors because they're those old people.

They're wrong.

Direct mail is not dead.[1] In fact, even organizations that have strong digital strategies rely on direct mail for the largest portion of the dollars they raise. Digital is catching up, but direct mail is still the big gorilla in most

---

[1] In all candor, I have often written about direct mail being dead because of the post office's crazy way of operating and because of how poorly some people use it. But in the right hands, direct mail is a powerful tool.

rooms. It is a time-tested and sturdy method for reaching donors. People are still opening envelopes, reading what they receive in their mailboxes, and responding to those messages.

Direct mail is one of the four major communication and relationship-building strategies used by nonprofits to raise money. The others include digital (such as email and social media), newsletters (either digital or direct-mail), and events. In most cases, direct mail is a letter or some other printed message addressed to an existing donor, a lapsed donor, or a potential new donor. For many nonprofits, direct mail is their most reliable fundraising tool.

While the digital space is always changing, with new technology for delivery and new metrics being added all the time, there have been fewer technological changes in direct mail. That alone is a testament to its durability. It's been used for decades by smart people, so there are some tried-and-true best practices that ensure it remains a valuable fundraising tool.

Direct mail is like a gas-powered car. It's tempting to think gas-powered cars are old technology. Why would you burn gas when you can get an electric vehicle or, someday, that flying car? Well, for most people who can afford the car and the gas, an automobile is still good technology, even though it's old. Cars are affordable for most, and you can get some that burn a lot less gas than cars used to burn. It's still the dominant form of personal transportation.

But, if you put a six-year-old behind the wheel of that car, it's not good technology. A 106-year-old driver? Not good technology. You put the wrong fuel in the car, it's not good technology. If you try to drive the car across the water, it won't be the right technology.

The same is true for direct mail; it only functions well if you use it properly.

START OUT RIGHT

A direct-mail campaign is only as good as who you're mailing (your database or list of donors and prospective donors). An effective campaign starts with two questions:

- ♥ Do you know who you are sending the letter to?
- ♥ Is it clear what you are asking the recipient to do?

Some people think that all they need to launch a direct-mail campaign is a mailing list and a letter. They need more than that. Before you start a campaign, you have to ask yourself, "Do I have accurate records? Do I have good names and addresses? Is my data clean? Do I know, for example, that this person goes by Steve? Do I know that Steve has a spouse named Kris and that she spells her first name with a K?"

One of our favorite stories is about a client who was renting lists on their own for a new donor acquisition project. One of the lists they rented was a pet owner's list, and unfortunately, the letters went out addressed to their pets.[2] I'm pretty sure the recipient knew the sender didn't know them when they received a fundraising letter addressed "Dear Fluffy." This is an obvious example, but it really illustrates the point of clean names in your database.

A donor can tell from your direct-mail letter if you know him. If you call him by the wrong name, you don't know him. If you spell his name wrong, you don't know him. If your letter is addressed to him "or current resident," then you obviously don't know him and don't care to get to know him. When these things happen, that letter is likely to get tossed into the garbage.

But if you know them, and they can see that you know them, they are much more likely to read your letter and get wrapped up in the story you want to tell them.

---

2   This is another situation I was concerned you'd think this was our mistake. For clarity (and to protect my self-esteem), the client was doing this project with a vendor, not us.

The second question, "Is it clear what I am asking them to do?" goes back to the communication scaffolding we talked about in chapter 4. You have to make it clear that you are asking them to participate with your organization. You are asking them to step up and help you solve a problem that is important to them.

If you can answer those two questions, you might be ready to use direct mail effectively.

Never think of your donor list as a mailing list. A mailing list really is a mass of faceless people. But your donors are individuals (even the businesses, corporations, and other organizations you might mail are composed of real, living people). If you think about your donors this way, you are more likely to deliver a letter that is warm, friendly, and knowledgeable—the kind of letter that's needed for direct mail to work. You're not writing to a group of people. You're writing to a person. As weird as it is to imagine, it's effective to imagine one person you are writing. Who are they? What do they look like? Why are they a donor? What are you asking them to do?

WHO TO HIRE

Direct-mail campaigns are complex and costly, so it makes sense to hire an expert to guide you. This is particularly true when you are making an appeal to potential new donors who you don't know well and who are not in your database. You're confident you can convince them to become donors, but the strategy and technical aspects of reaching them can be phenomenally tricky. No group should try to do that on its own.

You also want to be cautious about hiring a printer or a mailer to put this direct-mail campaign together for you. You want someone whose sole job is to connect with donors. This is not what a printer or mailing house is trained to do. Printers and mailers may say they can develop good potential donor lists, but this is a specialized skill that most printers and mailers don't have at the level of sophistication that you need.

Some businesses won't charge you for their creative and strategic work and only charge for their printing. The price tag may seem appealing, but the results are often worth what you paid for. That's why we tell our clients that the most expensive direct mail that you can send is stuff that looks like everyone else's. If the people you reach don't become donors or if they give once and disappear, the money you spent on that campaign is wasted.

You need a company that has worked on a variety of direct-mail appeals for organizations that are the same size as yours. Ask to see <u>samples of their work</u>. Is there a lot of <u>variety in their portfolio</u>, or is it all about the same thing? Have they done projects similar to what you have in mind? You don't want someone who offers quick answers. If they are going to succeed with your campaign, they need to spend some time with you. They need to become comfortable with what your organization is and who your donors are before they can be confident communicating on your behalf. And of course, ask about the results they're delivering for their clients.

Shy away from anyone who assures you that you will get an X percent return on your direct-mail appeal. We do millions of pieces of mail every year for clients, and I can predict to some degree what the response will be. But I also know enough to realize that there are always variables and surprises—both negative and positive—that will blow any prediction out of the water. So always be suspicious of someone who breezes into your first meeting and starts telling you exactly what you should do. To do the job right, your consultant has to fully understand your organization and who your donors are. That takes time.

It's analogous to hiring a doctor, lawyer, or accountant. You don't want to skimp. You want a professional with a good track record—someone who is going to do what is best for you, not just what you want to be done. You want someone to create a unique campaign for you and not something that they just did last week for XYZ nonprofit somewhere else in your town.

THE BEST WAY TO LOOK AT DIRECT MAIL

Some nonprofits think of direct mail as a panacea. It's going to fix all our fundraising problems, anybody can do it, and there will be legitimate returns on our investment.

However, there is no instant, genie-in-a-bottle solution. Direct mail is hard work, and like any sort of fundraising, the centerpiece is a strong message. Some say long letters are best, and others insist that only short letters work. The truth is there is no single right way to do it. We've had success for clients with very short letters and with long letters. The type of message you send depends on what your donors are used to and what you're asking from them. Your letter should reflect your desire to start or celebrate the personal relationship you have with that donor.

So, go at this with emotion. Start with a clear picture of the problem you are working on and allow the donor to see a way to make a difference by participating in this work with you. It's communicating within the scaffolding: stating the problem, the solution, the participation, and the consequences.

You also need a simple and convenient way for donors to respond to your appeal. Usually, that's a reply envelope that you've included in your letter. But you should also have a functioning website that allows donors to give quickly and securely online. Many donors, particularly those who don't have a relationship with you yet, will look at your website if they are thinking of donating. So, include your web address in the letter and make sure your website and letter's messaging is consistent so donors can instantly see that both were produced by the same organization. Ensure that the content of your letter is reinforced by what donors see on your website. And most importantly, in your letter, invite them to go online to learn more about you or to give a gift. That way the donor doesn't have to find a stamp or dig out their checkbook; they can easily give you a gift through your online giving portal.

When our clients use this approach, we actually see both digital and direct-mail responses increase. Donors like having a choice. Some will make a gift online the first time and then mail in a check the next time. It all depends on what's happening with them at that moment and what their motivation is. You have to make it easy for them to respond either way.

TECHNOLOGICAL ADVANCES WITH DIRECT MAIL

Direct mail, as I mentioned earlier, is a mature form of communication that hasn't changed much over the years. But recent technological developments have made it easier to tailor your direct-mail messages to discreet segments of your donor list.

For example, the version of the letter you send to major donors can be much different from the letter you send to potential new donors. The letter you send to lapsed donors can be different from the letter you send to major donors. The letter you send to supporters of your after-school program can be different from the letter you send to supporters of your summer school program. If a donor last supported your student backpack program three years ago, you might want to highlight that program as a way to reconnect them with the program that they first loved. You can also use different pictures within each segment of your donor list.

This kind of "versioning" is designed for distinct groups within your donor base but also for different behaviors, such as donors who give quarterly, or those who give every year in December, or those who give every other year. When you do this well, donors notice. They feel like you know them and care about them. They don't have qualms about donating because they trust you will receive it, validate it, and use their donation wisely.

New technology in digital printing allows great flexibility. Being able to create many versions of a single letter in a direct mail campaign a few years ago would have been far too expensive, but digital printing technology has made this more affordable and allows almost as much flexibility as an online format.

Your work continues even after the letter goes out. You have to track how much income comes in and how that amount compares to what you spent. The return on your investment will help you decide how to approach your next campaign.

Think about it as nourishing your donor database. Add your new donors. Note how your existing donors responded. Find out how many lapsed donors returned to the fold. This kind of detail will make your next direct-mail campaign (and any strategies) more effective.

Chapter Twelve

DIGITAL FUNDRAISING

Digital fundraising campaigns are like a mirage on the horizon. They seem impossibly alluring—the answer to all your fundraising needs. And just like some misinformed people think that direct-mail campaigns are dead, many people believe it's easy to raise money through digital channels, such as websites, email, and social media. The reality is that if you don't use digital strategies correctly, the mirage evaporates, as does your investment.

Without question, digital is the fastest-growing fundraising method for most organizations we serve. But it only works well when those digital channels are integrated into the fabric of the organization. A good example is something we talked about in the last chapter about direct mail. When you point people from your direct-mail piece to your website, and your website has some kind of connection to your direct-mail piece, with tools that allow visitors to learn more and donate, the two can work together to bring donations in.

The average gift from donors through a website is typically larger than the gifts we see coming in through direct mail. As a result, it often can be cheaper to raise money through the digital space than through direct mail. But it's not easy or automatic. And those economies work in your favor only after you have a great website and analytical tools in place. If your website doesn't stay focused on the donor and isn't geared toward creating strong donor relationships, it will be less effective than it could be. There are many ways to help donors feel comfortable giving online, and if you don't know those strategies and techniques, you may experience a painful lesson. The web strategies that work for your local insurance agent or car repair shop will not raise as much online revenue for you as doing the right kind of Donoricity digital strategies.

Digital channels are exciting to me because of the rich analytics they provide. We can see who opens our emails and how often. One of the tools we use for email allows us to watch emails as they are opened—you see names on a map. It is intoxicating to sit and watch results happen in real time.

We know what percentage of our emails are opened. We

can tell how many are visiting our websites, what geographic region they come from, how long they stay on the website, and which pages they read. All of that information helps us better understand our donors and assess strategies quickly.

Among the social media channels—Facebook, Twitter, Instagram, LinkedIn, and on and on—Facebook is the logical social media choice for most nonprofits. Facebook is where the most robust conversations helpful for most nonprofits are happening. Some argue that conversations are going on with LinkedIn, Twitter, and Instagram, but adults over thirty—your primary audience for potential donors—are primarily using Facebook. It's a place for relationships and connections. It's where people congregate. Until that changes, it's a good place for you to be.

THE PROBLEM OF EMAIL

Ironically, email is one of the most abused and at the same time underutilized digital strategies employed by nonprofits. When used properly, it is a powerful tool for reaching potential donors and validating gifts from supporters.

Our inboxes are one of the most intimate places for communication in modern society. It's where we get much of our important communications, and the messages there reach into every facet of our lives, from personal relationships to business associations. This makes email a glorious communication tool. It's just you and me in your inbox.

Email has so many uses for nonprofits. We use email to ask for help, just as we do in direct mail. We use email to provide feedback or to validate donors. We use email to allow donors to communicate back to us. We survey donors with email, alert them to important news, make big announcements, issue calls to action, and invite donors to events. It's versatile and inexpensive to use.

With the right tools, email campaigns are an easy way to reach a lot of people instantly with personalized messages. As a result, many overuse it and abuse recipients with unfocused or repetitive messages. Organizations abuse this channel more than any other by sending emails that don't provoke a donor's curiosity or invite them to be involved by volunteering or sharing their influence with other potential supporters. If potential donors think you're wasting their time, they will eventually hit the unsubscribe button, and that's the last thing you want them to do.

Although emails don't have the same inherent expense of a direct-mail piece—you don't need to buy postage or have your letter printed and stuffed in an envelope—they can be very expensive because of the regulations associated with email. If someone clicks to unsubscribe to your email, Congress says that you can't send them any more emails.[1] You're out of options. That asset of yours—that email address to the personal, quiet, and intimate inbox of a potential donor—is lost. That can be very costly, and it is the primary reason why nonprofits have to be careful not to overuse email. You have to respect the person who gave you their email. You must not over communicate. You have to communicate in a way that they will appreciate, with messaging that's important to them.

Emails allow you to test and refine your message. Email distribution software programs allow you to see who is opening your emails and how much time they are spending with them. We use a proprietary software to test our email campaigns. We test the length of our messages, the subject lines, the greeting—everything we can. Email programs allow you to play an analytics and strategy game. What are donors opening? What are they reacting to? How are they interacting with your message? And because you can see the data—almost live in real time—it allows you to communicate to a donor in a way that will be most engaging. It's like sitting across the table from someone and reading their body language and hearing their responses. It's magic if you know what you're doing.

---

1   If you're not sure about these rules, Google "CAN-SPAM Act" (such a great name).

It's important to integrate your email campaigns with your direct-mail campaigns. The idea is to send a similar but not identical message through both channels. Some might think that's redundant, but they actually work in concert to reinforce your central message. One channel serves as a reminder of the other channel. So when a donor gets a piece of mail from you, they might say, "I remember the email I got on this. Let's take a closer look," or vice versa. Or when they get the email, they'll remember the piece of mail they threw away without reading. So they support each other.

The two messages should have a similar look and similar phrases, and the illustrations or photos can be similar as well. When donors get to your website—the email and direct mail piece should both have a link or a web address—there ought to be similar words and elements so that donors know these channels are all connected. They know they're in the right spot. All of these elements stack up and become a powerful thing in the donor's mind.

CREATING A GREAT WEBSITE

If you're a nonprofit, the primary function of your website should be to raise money. That doesn't mean that all you have on your home page is big, red Donate button and then a credit card form on a donation page. But it does mean that you have to make it easy for visitors to get to the right page to donate. You have to make the donation page easy to identify and simple to use. If someone wants to donate to your organization, help them accomplish that goal with as few clicks as possible. Don't make them log in. Don't make them create a password. Please.

That doesn't mean you can't have other information on the website. You should. You should be telling your donors stories about lives they can change and the consequences of not addressing the problem at the center of your mission. But you have to make it clear what the ask is, and all the other pages on the site should be designed to support that primary goal of raising money. There are people out there who say you need to make people register and create a login and password in order to give a gift. Don't do it (my bias). Just flat out refuse. You want as few hurdles as possible. (Fair warning, this is not a favored strategy with most data-entry people, but that's OK.)

Many nonprofit websites are infuriating. They make it difficult to donate. You don't know where to go because someone thought a prominent donate button would be ugly or they wanted the donations page to blend in well with the rest of the site. Or they decided to name that button something cooler than "Donate" or "Give." If the primary purpose of your website is to raise money, why would you do anything to make it harder for people to do just that?

Many nonprofits have underperforming websites because they were designed by people who don't understand that the site's primary goal is to make it easy for people to donate money. Nonprofit websites are a narrow niche, and many web developers suffer from the "how hard can it be?" disease. They've designed lots of websites, and this one is just for a little nonprofit. So they think they can knock it out in no time, and the result is a brochure-type website better suited to a restaurant than a nonprofit organization.

We also see nonprofit websites designed by developers who thoroughly understand the technology but not the organization, so they design the website for people like them—people who can appreciate the latest cool features and design elements. But most donors don't need that. They like a professional, elegant design, but more importantly, they need the website to be easy to understand and navigate. If you want people to donate, make it easy. If you want people to volunteer, don't hide your volunteer page on some other interior page. It's easy to make a website so gloriously beautiful and complicated that people can't find the stuff they are looking for.

I cannot emphasize enough that you need to make sure

your website is mobile-friendly.[2] We have built tons of websites, and when we analyze our client's web analytics, we often see that more than half of their traffic comes from smartphones, tablets, and other mobile devices. The last thing you want, then, is web content that has to be pinched or zoomed so you can read it and fill out the form. Your website has to be instantly legible and functional on a small screen. That means fewer words, easy scanning, and clear-cut navigation tools. You can still have the contrasting colors and all the elements of good design but just on a small screen. Keep it simple.

When we do a website project for a client, we spend about 60 percent of our time planning the strategy and purpose of the site before we start moving pixels around. After giving the visitor an opportunity to give you a donation, what's the next most important thing visitors go to, and how does that connect to the primary function of the website? What kinds of questions do donors have in mind as they're giving, and do we make it easy for them to find answers to those questions?

We spend a lot of time looking at the analytics of our clients' former or existing websites. Which pages were the most popular, and which pages did visitors seem to

---

2   With today's web and design technology, your site should be able to handle mobile, tablets, laptops, and desktop screens without having a separate mobile site.

abandon quickly? What kind of searches did they conduct? You might find out that visitors are traipsing all over your website just trying to find out what your office hours are, so part of your plan, then, becomes making it easy to find the office hours. All the analysis helps you make decisions about how to design your new website.

After the website is up and running, monitor how people are actually using it. Are they using it the way you expected them to? If not, what is their behavior? There is almost always something unexpected, so you make some tweaks to make it go smoother—all with the goal of keeping the number of clicks to a donation as low as possible. This is careful design—not necessarily a pretty design in terms of fonts and colors and images, but a functional design that engages donors and gives them an opportunity to give as quickly and easily as possible.

Here's a simple, do-it-yourself method called the "Aunt Ruby test." Ruby was my mother's older sister, and we use her to imagine a nice, older woman who doesn't care about fancy website design. Sharp, but not super web-savvy. If you put someone like Aunt Ruby in front of a computer, could she quickly figure out who you are and how to give her gift? If it passes the Aunt Ruby test, you're good to go. If not, you need to think it over more.

When designing your website, don't get bogged down trying to develop a look or a message to appeal to a particular age group or generational group, like Millennials.[3] Millennials do support nonprofits, but because of their phase of life and other factors, they don't give at the same percentage as Baby Boomers and older people. The older generations simply have more disposable income. The moment you start chasing one particular age group, you leave another group behind. You lose an opportunity to develop great relationships with a large group of donors that has disposable income and an inclination to give.

At the time I'm writing this book, our clients are seeing triple the national benchmarks for online income growth. Many of our clients are seeing this exponential growth over the national averages three and four years in a row.

That growth comes from our singular focus to make it easy for a potential donor to give a gift on that website. That goal guides everything we create. Everything is focused on making it easy for donors to give or get involved in some way. Designing a website that accomplishes this is not simple, and it's not an automatic return. But when it's done right, it's a thing of beauty.

---

3   I keep mentioning the Millennials because of how many times I encounter misguided strategies to connect with this group.

SOCIAL MEDIA

While websites should be designed to help you raise money, Facebook is not a good tool for that.

Instead, Facebook allows you to have conversations about your cause and the problems you're solving. It's never a good idea to use it to lecture donors, but it's an excellent way to celebrate the success your donors are having by working with your group. Currently, Twitter, Instagram or LinkedIn are not as good at doing this, so we generally tell our clients to not focus on those and other channels that are too limited to allow for a nuanced or deep discussion. The moment we publish this book, the digital world will have changed. It's just moving so fast. Connect with me on the Donoricity site to learn the most up-to-date strategies for digital.

Facebook can be a powerful way to support your fundraising, however. One of our clients had a strong online income through their website, and since they weren't raising any money through Facebook, they decided to stop investing time in communicating with their donors that way. Posting regularly on Facebook took up too much time, and since there seemed to be no return on that investment, they cut back.

What we noticed was that their online income, which had

been going up month over month, started to decline in almost an exact parallel with the decline in their engagement on Facebook. The less interaction our client had with donors on Facebook, the less people gave online.

At first, it didn't make sense; the organization wasn't asking people to give on Facebook, so why would that cause their income to drop at the same rate?

Here's why: Facebook was where they were talking about their life and work. That's where they were helping donors understand their cause. That's where they were showing the positive results that came from their work and where they were giving donors feedback. It was also where the organization had been talking about the consequences of not addressing the problem that they were working on. In other words, their Facebook page was a key place for them to talk about the four elements of their scaffolding: the problem, the solution, the participation, and the consequences. When they went silent, donors got distracted. Donors didn't have as much chance to engage with the organization and understand the problem and the solutions to it. Donors no longer had an opportunity to spread their influence because the organization's Facebook page no longer gave them the stories that they wanted to share. They lost that frequency of messaging that creates the top-of-mind awareness that's so vital.

This illustrates why it's important to use your communication scaffolding on social media (really everywhere). You wouldn't try to incorporate all four elements into each post, but you can mix and match those elements as a way of continually communicating with your donors and allowing them to communicate with others.

We worked with one client who helps people in poverty. We were trying to illustrate that people in poverty are not always unemployed; a lot of people experiencing poverty work hard at low-paying jobs and struggle to make ends meet. So we did a post on Facebook that calculated the astounding number of hours a week someone would have to work at a fast-food restaurant to make enough money to pay the average cost of an apartment in that part of the country.

The post provoked a fascinating discussion on Facebook. Some people didn't believe it, of course, while others were outraged, and some just shrugged it off. But the discussion served to increase our client's visibility. It was one way for us to get people's attention and get them thinking about this problem and whether it was the kind of problem they wanted to work on with our client.

What makes Facebook so powerful is its ability to spread ideas and capture people's attention.

Oh, and for clarity, we almost never directly solicit donations via social media. Our digital team calls it "talking around the ask, not making the ask." Resist the urge to do too much asking for gifts on Facebook. The social space of Facebook is best for conversations, validations, and connections.

Chapter Thirteen

NEWSLETTERS: DIGITAL AND PRINT

I have colleagues who believe organizations should use newsletters only to thank donors. I disagree. As I've already said, thanking donors is much less effective than validating their support by showing them the tangible results of their contributions. I think newsletters, both print and digital, are an opportunity to reconnect donors with this great cause that your organization is about. Take a deep breath; I never produce a newsletter that doesn't have a call to action in it. And usually, that call to action is a financial ask. When we do this, we can sometimes raise more dollars with a newsletter that we do with direct appeals. We typically don't do as many newsletters as we would direct-mail or digital appeals, but newsletters are a great way to help donors understand the need and the opportunities for them to become involved.

Newsletters give you more real estate to tell a compelling story. It might be a story about someone you've helped or a problem the organization has worked on, and a newsletter allows you to go into more detail and create a narrative that pulls the donor in. A mistake some nonprofits make is using the extra real estate in a newsletter to cram in a story about their canned food drive and a secondary article featuring a list of the board of directors. That's usually a mistake. A better approach is to focus on the central narrative so that you are taking the donor on a journey to help them understand this great problem you are solving and how they can be a part of it.

CONTENT

Donors are busy, so you want to keep the narrative and the newsletter itself clean and focused. It's best to have one deeper story about a person or a situation, and then supporting information that expands on that central theme. Include a column with some heartfelt words from your leader that connects back to and explores one aspect of that central story. That column can also explain why this person or this situation is not unique; it's part of a larger, ongoing problem that continues to need work.

You need to put a human face on the organization.[1]

---

1   Assuming you help people.

It's also important to have a piece on how people can become involved by donating, volunteering, or spreading the word about the organization. Many nonprofits have a "Did you know?" kind of column, but that feature feels overdone. Instead, I like columns like "Here are five things you should know about this problem," or "Here are three things to tell your friends about us." Sometimes there's even greater power in creating your list of what you are not. "We don't just give handouts, we equip people to work," or "No, you can't come see the elephants; we're a sanctuary not a zoo." It's unexpected and surprising. It's essentially the same thing as "Did you know?" but it's a different approach that can help you avoid that pattern blindness we talked about in chapter 7. You don't want to have the same content over and over again. Mix it up. I personally love "Three things to tell your friends about us" because it suggests to your donors that they should do just that, and it gives them the material they need to do it.

Newsletters that are no more than four pages get read more, and donors respond to them better than anything larger than that. We recommend that newsletters go out at least four times a year and usually no more than six times, but your situation is unique and your mileage will vary.

I also recommend newsletters that are highly visual. We use infographics and a lot of images and icons; roughly

66% PICS   *33% TEXT*

two-thirds of our newsletters are images (and whitespace) and the other third is text. That's because people will rarely sit down with your newsletter, put on their reading glasses, adjust the light, and settle in for a nice read. It's more likely that they will just scan the newsletter. Try to convey the story in headlines, subheads, pull quotes, pictures, and captions. Like I said before, infographics are a great way to tell a story or provide the context or background for the situation your story talks about.

One strong idea is to feature donors in your newsletter. These articles should not brag about the donor's gift but should give other donors ideas for participating in ways they haven't considered before. We've done stories on donors who made significant estate gifts. These pieces allow donors to talk about why that gift was rewarding and how it helped the charity make progress toward solving a specific problem. I can recall a profile of a couple that focused not on the gift the donors made but on how the husband and wife were trying to show their daughters the value of giving. These articles inspire other donors.

I've also seen profiles of board members, staffers, and other people who support an organization at a high level. It's also effective to interview regular rank-and-file donors, like the sweet, little, retired librarian who is giving not because she has great wealth but because she has a great commitment.

Be careful to not focus only on big dollar donors. You don't want your smaller donors to get the impression that you only care about people who give big money. If you are featuring a donor who's giving a significant amount of money, concentrate on the heart of the donor not the dollars. And please, don't do one of those big check photos. Those only send the message that you're about big checks.

As always, it's important to keep the focus off of the organization and on the people or creatures or whatever you are helping. If you're doing a newsletter story on your new building, make it about what goes on in that building to help solve this problem you are all working on.

DELIVERING THE NEWSLETTER

It's a good idea to send out your newsletter in an envelope rather than a self-mailer with a label on it. It will cost a little more, but the envelope sends a message that the newsletter has value. A newsletter mailed directly with a label won't feel important to the recipient, and they're more likely to throw it away without opening it.

I also include a cover letter with the newsletter. This surprises some people, but the letter is usually the first thing people read, so it functions as a teaser for the newsletter. For example, you might say, "You don't want to miss our story of Angela, who was able to turn her life around with your help." If the newsletter gets tossed unread, the letter gives you another chance to communicate with a potential donor.

Let recipients know, either on the envelope or in the letter, that you're enclosing their newsletter. It's important to be upfront about that. You don't want to surprise them, and you don't want them to think it's something it's not. It's also an opportunity to reinforce with donors that it's their newsletter talking about what they accomplished with their support.

Your newsletter should always ask the donor or the reader to participate by giving. Provide them with volunteer opportunities as well as the chance to donate money.

NEWSLETTER DESIGN

It's good practice to redesign your newsletter every couple of years. You don't want to change the look so dramatically that donors are confused and don't recognize you, but you can still change the physical dimensions or format of the newsletter. If donors have been exposed to four to six newsletters a year for the last two or three years, change up the look a bit and put a little attention speed bump in there. You can adjust the colors or update the fonts. Change physical dimensions. With some clients with robust newsletter schedules, we'll produce a special edition with a different shape and physical size. Those usually perform well because it breaks the pattern slightly. You want it to look familiar, but you also want to keep it fresh.

Your newsletter isn't a magazine, but its look should be closer to a slick magazine than to those classic newsletters of yesterday, with their jagged photos, long sections of text, and dated or amateurish fonts. You want it to look like it was designed in this century, and you want it designed so people can read it quickly and easily and still get a clear message. You have to make wise choices about things like font size and line spacing and kerning and indents and subheads—all those typographic choices that can make the material easier to consume.

? why

Some groups give their newsletter a name. I don't think a donor cares what you call it, but it's OK to have a name for your piece.

DIGITAL NEWSLETTERS

Your digital newsletter should never have exactly the same

content as your print version. Don't ever let anyone talk you into just saving your print newsletter as a PDF and posting on your website and calling it a digital newsletter. Downloaded PDFs are a source of computer virus problems, so you don't want to give your donors that experience. Also, a lot of people have software that prevents them from downloading things. What's more, downloaded PDFs are not easy to read on a mobile device, and that's how many donors access your website.

The ideal approach is to create a separate digital newsletter that carries the same central message as your print newsletter but has less text and includes links that donors can follow to get more about the story they're interested in. You might have a photo with a little bit of copy and a link to the full story. These links should take them to your website, where you can tell the rest of the story and share additional photos. Once they're on your website, you can use your analytics to see which stories they spent the most time with, which ones they ignored, and how many pages they visited altogether. This is all valuable information that helps you improve the content of future e-newsletters.

Send donors both the digital and the print versions of your newsletter. Deliver them a week or so apart so they don't both arrive on the same day. You are not trying to bludgeon your donors with information, but keep in mind that not everyone who reads your emailed newsletter will read your printed newsletter and vice versa. But even if they did, that's good reinforcement of your message. People who don't make a donation after the first newsletter might be convinced to give when they receive the second.

The digital version is also the place to tell the longer story that didn't fit into your print version. Online, your writer can spend more time unpacking a story, although you still have to be aware of your donors' limited attention spans. Don't fall in love with your own words; make sure the online story accommodates scanners and provides links to those who want to read more about something.

Your newsletter should be a great involvement device. Allow people to easily reach your donation page. Provide good links to more information. Allow them to comment, ask questions, or send you an email. When talking about volunteering, provide the link to a sign-up page. The goal is to make it clear what you are asking for and where donors can go for more information.

The goal isn't to use your newsletter as a way to say "thank you." Thanking donors misses the point of why people give. Instead, look for ways to make people feel good for supporting you and working with you. The goal is to validate your donors and give them a chance to participate further (apologies for continuing to say this over and over). If you've done a good job with your newsletter, the donor will be thinking, "I've got to do some more of this. I've got to help some more." You don't want to miss that opportunity to get a donor involved more fully.

Some nonprofits feel awkward about making this kind of an appeal in their newsletters. They have the mistaken idea that donors don't want to give or that donors need to be persuaded to give. Nothing could be further from the truth. If you tell a good story about the people they've helped or the problem they have contributed to solving, and you pack that story with emotion, keeping the donors' feelings foremost in your mind, your donors will want to help more. They may not be able to make a donation at that time, so that's when you say, "Come on down and volunteer!" or "We'll give you a tour!" or "Here are three things to tell your friends about us."

Another problem with just saying "thank you" is that it infers that the job has been completed. There is the suggestion of an ending. It's like you are saying, "Thanks for my birthday present! See you next year!" You don't want that because your work continues, and you are going to need donors' help throughout the year.

How often can you email your donors? We had one client

who insisted we could email their donors no more than twice a month. If we did more than that, they thought, their donors would unsubscribe and they would lose them. If we were sending the same messages over and over again, that would be a legitimate fear. But we found that when we use variety in our messaging, people were happy to hear from us. We found that we could send a great deal more emails, raise a ton of money, and not have the unsubscribe numbers go up at all.

Chapter Fourteen

MAJOR DONORS

Some organizations spend a lot of time trying to define what "major donor" means. How many dollars a year do you have to give to be a major donor? There's no magic number that makes you a major donor. A major donor for a small organization might be considered a midlevel or general donor to a much larger organization.[1]

Think about it this way: A major donor is simply a donor of significance. The dollar level they're giving at makes them rarer than most of your donors. There is not specific dollar level that signifies that someone is a major donor; what's important is that their gift is conspicuously large compared to most of the gifts you receive. They are people who, when the hot water heater goes out or the intern

---

1   Without a doubt, this is the most common and consistent question I am asked about major donors.

MAJOR DONOR BASIS

crashes the van, you can call up and ask for help. They are people you connect with on the phone, via personal email, or through live, handwritten notes with stamps and everything. They are people who are typically faithful, have given large gifts, and have demonstrated a capacity to write a large check.

NOT CUME

When identifying major donors, we consider their capacity rather than the frequency of their gifts. For instance, you can have a donor who gave you five thousand dollars, but they reached that number by giving you a series of fifty-dollar donations over the course of several years. That's an amazing donor, but you don't want to consider them a major donor. They likely don't have the capacity to give larger amounts, even though their gifts add up and their contributions are vital to your organization.

Some organizations use data tools called "wealth overlays" or "wealth indicators" to identify potential major donors. These are data tools that identify a person's giving capacity based on what amounts to a credit check. Their magic data machines run some numbers and come back with a list of people who have giving capacity and a history of supporting other nonprofits. They also suggest how much you can ask them to donate.

The problem is that these tools are often more general and

inaccurate than you'd expect. I've looked at the report they spit out about me, and it was both hilarious and sad how far off they were. They had me associated with companies I'd never heard of and missed companies that I own. What's more, they were inaccurate in their estimation of my wealth.

The other problem—and the most significant problem with these wealth overlays—is that they give no indication of philanthropic intent. You may get the name of a potential donor, and you may learn that they donated a hundred thousand dollars to XYZ Cancer Society. But that information has zero bearing on whether they would be interested in donating to you. I worked with one large national organization that ignored its own donors in its database so it could chase after these mythical, wealth-laden unicorns. They pursued the theory and ignored the reality of their donors' behavior, many of whom had great capacity for giving and had already demonstrated their love for the organization.

On another occasion, I had a development officer tell a couple who supported a ministry that he felt they were making a poor giving decision by donating so much. This couple lived very quietly in a modest home, and what the development officer didn't realize was that they had chosen to live that way so that they could have greater capacity to support the causes they believed in. In their minds, God did not want them to have a fancy house. He wanted them to use their wealth to right wrongs in the world.

The point here is that it's a mistake to treat major donors like you are making a sales call and have inside knowledge of their bank accounts. What's more important is knowing what is in that donor's heart. What they value is not determined by their wealth, salary, or net worth. Wealth overlays can be terrific tools to provide some perspective on your donors. Just remember that these data profiles are no substitute for knowing a donor and tracking the donor's actual behavior.

Groups that try to find and cultivate major donors quickly learn that people of great wealth have staff members whose job is to keep groups like them away. The whole world is trying to get a meeting with these wealthy people, and if they don't want to see you, you are not going to get an appointment. The trick, then, is to connect with people who are already in your database or who are wealthy friends of people in your database. Allow your contacts and connections to grow naturally. Don't go for the pie in the sky; you're stepping over people who are already writing you checks and providing for you right now. Those people may continue to give and may increase their giving.

In Texas, we say, "Dance with them that brung ya." Go with people who have an affinity for you and have already raised their hand and said, "I want to be involved." See how you can deepen that relationship and their desire to work with you. That's the place to put your energy.

Major donors, no matter how you define them, give for the same reasons that other donors give: because they want to make the world a better place. A major donor is still a person. While he or she may be putting several zeroes at the end of their gift, they are still an emotionally driven person, and they want to be sure that their donation is going to have a significant, material impact.

COMMUNICATING TO MAJOR DONORS

While it's true that you may communicate differently to major donors than other donors, never create major donor brochures and proposals that look like investment materials with calculations of investment returns and the like. Some nonprofits think that since these are financially successful people, they are expecting to see these glossy investment prospectuses.

In my experience, that is not the case. Major donors, like other donors, want to change lives or have a large impact of their community. The only difference may be that, while some donors hope to change one person's life, a major donor may have the capacity to change an entire village or town's life. The mistake that's easy to make is trying to appeal to someone who expects you to run the numbers on their investment. In fact, most major donors are just like you and me and just want to help someone out. They want to make a difference in the world.

Communicate with major donors in any way they will allow. If they are coffee-and-pie people, have coffee and pie with them. If they prefer email, use email. Each is an individual, so learn their behaviors and be sensitive to their preferences. You might ask, "Is this the right email to use?" or "Is it OK if I call you?" Be respectful. About the worst thing you can do is show up at someone's front door without calling first and expect him to have a conversation with you.

Major donors should get all the communications that the rest of your donors get, although these newsletters, direct-mail pieces, and email communications should be "versioned" so they make sense to the recipient. Just as you would not say the same thing to a faithful donor that you would say to someone who has never given, your communication to a major donor has to reflect the role they play in your organization. The receipting and validation are just as important, but the appeal for their income, influence, or involvement must reflect their importance to your organization.

One of the tragic mistakes I see is when a nonprofit board member or an executive decides a major donor should no longer receive routine communications. Since major donors typically get more personal, face-to-face communication with your organization, the belief is that other forms of communication like emails or direct mail will only irritate or offend them. Even a carefully crafted version of that direct mail can be seen as too much.

But what we've seen is that those donors' giving goes down when you restrict routine communication like that. We ran a test where half of our client's major donors got special treatment, and communication was restricted to face-to-face contact. The other half of the client's major donors received versions of the same direct mail and emails other donors were getting. Time after time, giving was higher among the latter group—those who received all the communications, as well as the personal contacts. The moral of this story is that your well-meaning desire not to overwhelm your major donors can cause them to forget you.

PULLING BACK THE CURTAIN

Acknowledge your major donors as insiders who are

making significant gifts. Allow them to be heroes and champions because they are doing great good. Don't ask them to make a donation every time you communicate with them. Instead, pull back the curtain on your organization and share with them important developments in your nonprofit.

Major donors need access to senior executives in your organization. They need to hear your big dreams and plans. Your vision and the strategies you're using are powerful tools to inspire them.

With our rescue mission clients, we communicate with their major donors in the early fall to give them a heads up about what our needs are going to be and what kind of discussions and strategies we'll be engaging in over the coming months. We are frank with them. We tell them that we will need to feed a lot more people than the previous year, and we alert them that we will be asking for help. With those impacts, we are not specifically asking for donations, but we are sharing insider information and letting them think about what they would like to support and how much they would like to give when they get the ask piece.

Special events and tours are another way to pull back the curtain. It's common for many nonprofits to have special events just for major donors. We've had major donors come as a group to our client's rescue mission to serve meals restaurant style to homeless people. That kind of bonding and emotional experience will change the donor. It's an experience you can't have unless you are on the inside.

We've found that major donors love to know the inside information and to have things explained to them. They appreciate the organization's respect, and as a result, they give more. Because of their commitment, the organization shares more information with them and donors feel a closer bond. The next time we ask them to give, they have some memory of how they felt, and they feel good about giving again.

THE PERSONAL APPROACH

Most major donors expect some contact with the non-profit's leader, but many CEOs don't feel like they have the time. We advise them to find the time; major donors expect it and they respond better when they have more connection with the organization's CEO.

There is no one better to connect with a donor over a significant dollar gift than the executive leadership. Administrative assistants and development officers can help keep a major donor informed and close to the organization, but when it comes to asking for a that huge gift for your next project, that should come from the executive leadership.

In reality, every nonprofit leader handles this contact differently. Sometimes, board members help by contacting or connecting with major donors. Whatever approach you use, it's important to remember that major donors should be allowed to have a line of communication and some live person to respond to their questions, give them validation, or connect them with the cause. Many donors are not looking for a lot of contact, but they need that relationship so that they can hear the stories.

With major donors, big vision is critical. They need to hear the human-level story about the person who was helped thanks to their donation, but sometimes that human level is elevated. You're talking about the village that was saved, the school that was built, the river that was cleaned up. If they are business people or people of great wealth or wherewithal, that kind of grander scale fits who they are.

Chapter Fifteen

WRAPPING UP

First, I want to say "thank you" for wading all the way through the book. Even if you just flipped to the last chapter to see how it ends, I'm grateful. I've been blessed to work in and around nonprofits and ministries for a big chunk of my life. I love you crazy dreamers who do this work. I appreciate your passion and dedication. This book might help you change the world.

I also want to remind you that you can do this.

Sure, if you do Donoricity strategies right and do them in a large organization with many donors and complex cultivation strategies, it's tricky. But at its core, this is about connecting your organization with the heart of a donor.

I know that if you concentrate on connecting with donors,

focus on tapping into their passions, emphasize stories, and boldly inject emotion into your work, you will see a difference. A big difference.

You may have to shift your work completely. But I doubt it. There are probably elements of the Donoricity strategies you're already doing, but you're also probably still being rather organization-focused in other areas.

Experiment. Figure out how Donoricity fits your situation and context.

You'll find your way.

LET'S GO BACK TO THE DONORS

Walk back with me into that Starbucks we visited in chapter 2. Remember the young man who finally worked up the nerve to sit with the woman he'd been watching across the coffee shop? All he could talk about was himself and how his mother used to make him lattes with cinnamon and nutmeg. The girl finally got up and left.

What if our poor friend had thought a little more about the woman who interested him? What if he asked about her tastes? When did she start drinking lattes? Did she ever put cinnamon or nutmeg on it? The woman warms up a bit. She likes to put honey in her lattes. Her dad raises bees and collects his own honey. The young man tries it and loves it! This changes everything, he says. "I didn't think it was possible, but you taught me an entirely different way to enjoy my morning lattes."

She's not leaving now. She's not as enthusiastic about coffee as her new friend, but she does feel good knowing she helped the guy out. "If you don't have any honey, a drop of vanilla is also good in lattes," she says.

Donor relationships flourish in the same way.

You can't always enjoy a latte with your donors, but you can help them recognize how they have made a big difference in the world. When you do that, they will stay with you and want to help even more.

LET'S CONNECT

I'm finishing this chapter sitting on the deck at home because the office was crazy with a creative meeting. I wanted to think about you for this last part. And I just deleted all the traditional conclusion and wrapping-up language I'd drafted. Really, you don't need me to tell you what I've told you. You're smarter than that.

I've also thought of three major topics I can't believe I left out. But if I don't wrap this up and call it done, I'll never finish. So, if you've gotten to the end, and you can't believe I didn't mention X, I understand. I'm with you.

Our new website, Donoricity.com, is up and running. You and I can connect on all the things I didn't have room for in this book (or didn't think about until it was too late). I'll be putting resources there you can download. You can also find out about our work and what we do.

When we trademarked "It's all about relationships" as part of Oneicity's brand, we really meant it. I would absolutely love to hear about you and your work.

If you have questions, ask. And if I can help you, let's talk. You can find out how to connect with me at Donoricity. com.

Now, put the book down and go raise some money. You have a world to change.

ACKNOWLEDGEMENTS

My thanks go to my clients who blessed me with the opportunity to get to know them and to serve them. The world is a better place because you are pushing back the darkness, caring for people, reducing suffering, and loving donors. Let's do this some more!

In particular, our client and my friend Jeff Gilman shaped Donoricity through our conversations and through his thoughtful perspective about his ministry's donors.

Thanks also to the Oneicity team who had to first put up with years of vague, unfocused, unproductive talk from me about my desire to write about this magic we're doing. And then when I finally figured out how to get it done, you had to put up with my preoccupation and lack of responsiveness during the time it took to grind it out.

Thanks for your patience (or pretended patience). I'm proud to work with each and every one of you. You are the very best in the business.

Profound gratitude goes to my beloved Hoots: business partner, coconspirator, partner in all things, and wife. I never could have done it without your reading my incoherent copy, wading through my crazy ideas, and continuing to believe this could ever amount to anything. I am grateful for and amazed by you.

Finally, I need to say publicly, thank you to God for the blessings and opportunities I've been given. My heart and life are full.

Desperately needed help for this project came from a variety of kind, generous, crazy-talented people. In particular, thank you to Kathleen, Jim, and Tom. You were always the right people at the right time.

Of course, any mistakes, errors, or inaccuracies are entirely mine. I did my best to tell it straight while protecting confidences where it seemed wise.

STEVE THOMAS
NOVEMBER 2017

ABOUT THE AUTHOR

For more than twenty years, **STEVE THOMAS** has lead nonprofits out of financial crisis mode and into unprecedented growth by helping them embrace donor-focused messaging and sound financial strategy. A former nonprofit CEO, Thomas consulted for a wide range of nonprofits, from start-ups to some of the largest Christian ministries. He is a partner in two advertising agencies, Oneicity, which works with Christian ministries, and Hoots & Thomas, which serves nonprofits and small businesses. He lives on Bainbridge Island, Washington, with his wife and partner, Kris Hoots. You can find out more about their work at www.donoricity.com.

Clients
Love 146

Redwood Gospel Mission
Jeff Gilman

p 97 ✓ IRS TY Rec
p 30 - Dominicity.com

48250982R00125